finding **Joi**

A True Story of Faith, Family, and Love

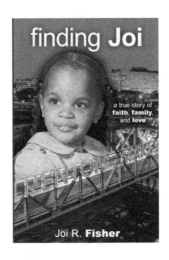

BY
Joi R. Fisher

Unless otherwise noted, Scripture quotations are from the Holy Bible, New International Version, copyright © 1973, 1978, 1984 by International Bible Society. Used with permission of Zondervan.

Printed in the United States of America
2018 First Edition
10 9 8 7 6 5 4 3 2 1

Subject Index:
Fisher, Joi R
Title: Finding Joi: A True Story of Faith, Family, and Love
1. Adoption 2. Education 3. Education Administration 4. New Jersey Legislation 5. Adoptee Birthright Bill 6. The College of New Jersey 7. Kean University

Paperback ISBN: 978-1-7336314-0-2
Library of Congress Card Catalog: 2019901181

www.findingjoi.us
MindThrive Publishers L.L.C.
www.mindthrivepublishers.com

Praises for Finding Joi...

"I was comforted as I kept thinking, *You felt that way, too, Joi*? As different as our experiences were as relinquished and adopted people, a lot of what we felt was the same. The deep seriousness of this memoir is threaded through with anecdotes that bring both tears and laughter. I am so glad that Joi took the time to chronicle her journal so carefully so that she could share it with us."
Pam Hasegawa, Spokesperson,
NJ Coalition for Adoption Reform and Education

"Joi Fisher's memoir is one of the most insightful books of an adoptee's journey that I have ever read. Joi speaks to her experiences on so many levels that it is a MUST READ for everyone touched by adoption (Adoptees, Adoptive parents, Birth parents, siblings, etc.). I couldn't put it down!"
Tom McGee
Co-facilitator, Morristown Post Adoption Support Group
Adoption Activist, NJCARE (New Jersey Coalition for Adoption Reform)

"I have known Joi for quite a some time but was not aware that she was adopted until a couple of years ago. Through reading her book, I found her story to be rather fascinating. Through her pen, I walked along her journey with her. Her story is one of a compelling complete self-discovery. Not only is it a fascinating read, but there are a plethora of lessons for the non-adopted reader to take away as well."
Principal Baruti Kafele
Educator / Author

"I love reading about adopted people helping each other. Joi's book will help others by passing along so honestly the lessons she's learned."
Penny Callan Partridge
Co-founder in 1973 of Adoption Forum of Philadelphia

"Bravo! Joi's honest, moving story of self-discovery, adoption and re-union is a moving, important addition of books by and about the adoption experience written by adopted people themselves.
Alison Larkin, Comedienne, award-winning audiobook narrator, and bestselling author of *The English American*, a novel

"*Finding Joi* is filled with heartfelt questions, everyday situations, and emotions, that shed light on the myriad of challenges adoptees face in searching for answers to our existence. Although the journey of every adoptee is different, the similarities are uncanny; whether male or female, young or old, adoptees knowledge of our birth parents and family history are critical to healing, forgiveness and filling the constant void in our lives. Joi's story resonated with me on many levels and I am grateful to have connected with her. Regardless of success, accolades, or stature, at the end of the day, all adoptees want to know, "Who Am I Really?" I hope that Joi's story encourages other adoptees to share their truth and find peace in their discovery."
Damon Davis
Host, "Who Am I... Really?" Podcast

Dedication

*To all of those who hide behind the veil of secrecy in a bad relationship, live in fear, struggle with identity, have fears of abandonment, are not sure how you are going to make it... this story is for YOU. From living in the Twilight Zone to Finding Joi, Love, and Peace. It is **never** too late. Finding Joy is POSSIBLE!*

Table Of Contents

Praises For Finding Joi… III

Dedication v

Bless Me ix

Preface..x

Lesson One - The Joy Of Learning 1

1 The "A" Word.. 3

2 The Ties That Bind 6

3 Spitting Image 16

4 Model Behavior 25

5 Unknown 35

6 Faith Walk 40

7 Forever Family 46

8 Close Encounters 49

9 Stir up the Gift 57

Lesson Two - The Joy Of Motherhood, Marriage & Divorce........ 65

10 It's Official!.. 67

11 Drugs, Lies, and Divorce....................................... 78

12 My Girls Say the Darndest Things 89

13 Superwoman 96

14 As the Girls Turn 104

Lesson Three - The Joy Of Education.. 113

    15 A Song for Education 115

    16 Things They Don't Teach in School 117

    17 A Call to Do Better.. 124

Lesson Four - The Joy Of Connection..................................... 127

    18 80 Questions 129

    19 Spitting Image Part 2
    The First Reunion... 138

    20 A Tall Order 151

    21 A Window of Opportunity 165

Lesson Five - The Joy Of Love 175

    22 Full Circle.. 177

    23 Second Time Around... 180

    24 Letters to My Girls.. 185

    Acknowledgments 194

    The Apple Doesn't Fall Far From The Tree........................... 199

    The Joy Of Great Memories 201

    My Girls 229

    Adoption Timeline 244

    My Confirmation.. 257

    About The Author 264

    For Bookings & More Information 266

Bless Me

I'm not sure if you can see
How the pressures of life fall on me
I don't know where I'm supposed to be or
Comprehend the Master's vision for me
I'm beginning to realize the strengths within me
I continue to ask for guidance from thee

Lord lead me, guide me, help me see
The beautiful seeds you planted in me
Mold me, shape me, help me see
Everything you'd have me be

As I bow down on bended knee
I ask you father to bless me

Bless Me

- Joi R. Fisher

Preface

"Growing up, I convinced myself that being adopted didn't bother me because I had such a great family. But the reality of it is that great parents do not erase the fact my birth parents gave me away."

Adoptees look in the mirror every day and the best guess we have as to our ethnicity is what we see in the mirror. My parents knew my mom was Black. I knew I was Black on the surface, but so much of who we are is also tied to our ethnicity. I was concerned because if I did not know my identity, then my kids don't fully know who they are either, except for what they see on the surface. Apparently, my surface has left people wondering. Ethnic history is very important. I recall heading south on a road trip and stopped at a gas station one summer and when the attendant asked me, "What country are you from?" I was startled and replied, "America." He gave me a look as if to say, *I don't believe you.* Later that same day, I stopped in a corner store and the cashier started talking to me in Spanish. At first, I didn't realize that she was speaking to me. Then she and the guy at the register stared at me and she asked, "What country are you from?" The two of them went back and forth between what South American country I was from to various islands in the Caribbean. I replied, "I'm Black and from New Jersey!" They immediately became defensive and shook their heads at me in disgust. The woman then shouted, "No Mami, you are not Black!" *Now, what in the world am I supposed to say to that*? I thought to myself. For some reason, encounters like this happen often. Some days I reply, " I don't know." Other times I make something up. Yet on the days when I want to tell what I know, "I'm Black!" I get pushback. Everyday life presents constant reminders that I don't know who I really am on the inside. As an adoptee, I have always had this overwhelming desire to find out my identity. *Finding Joi* is not just a play on words or an oxymoron; it is my truth, my journey to find the missing links to my biological roots.

My husband and I separated in 2013. Throughout most of 2014, we were back and forth in court. I remember being anxious to make it to Watch Night service at First Baptist Church to ring in the 2015 New Year. I have always enjoyed bringing in the New Year in church. Even though I had begun therapy a year prior, at times, I felt like I was on the brink of a nervous breakdown. Every aspect of my personal and professional life had finally come to a crisis point. I realized that I was in desperate need of divine intervention. Although I have been in church my entire life and prayed often, I was doubting God. My faith was being tested like never before. Being in a church that evening was the only thing that felt right.

My toxic marriage of over 19 years finally ended in divorce in 2015. I was relieved, angry, and broken. After all those years I recognized that I had allowed my ex-husband to psychologically manipulate and control every aspect of my being. I was free from making excuses for a blatant liar and drug abuser. I was free from the gut-wrenching yelling and outbursts. I was free from second-guessing my sanity. Yes, I was free from Gary — so I thought.

Yet, the trigger points from that dysfunctional relationship continued to set me back. I was trying to hold down my responsibilities as a mother to my three daughters who were in high school and college while juggling two administrative roles as a founding member of a newly-formed charter high school. All while dealing with years of insecurity over my differences and feelings of not fitting in with those close to me. I felt alone often. I had no one who could relate to my self-doubt regarding body frame, mannerisms, deep voice, quirkiness, and the huge void in my heart that constantly looped questions of *why* I was given up for adoption. *Was I not good enough*?

On May 27, 2014, Governor Chris Christie of New Jersey signed historic legislation, The Adoptees' Birthright Act (P.L. 2014, C. 9). This new law grants adopted New Jerseyans born after November 14, 1940 access to their original birth certificates (OBC) *without* a court order. My parents had been sending me information about this legislation for years and in 2014, it was finally enacted. The law would not take effect until January 1, 2017, but it was a personal victory for me and thousands like me in our state who desired more identifying information about our birth. I was not a fan of Governor Christie, but when the law went into effect, he became my hero. Not one to waste time, I nervously and excitedly applied for my OBC on January 9, 2017.

It was no secret in the extended Fisher family that I was adopted at two months old. I've known that I was adopted since I was a kindergartner. My mom always presented to me that my birth mother loved me enough to give birth to me and knew that she couldn't take care of me. For whatever reason, she chose to make sure a family was able to raise me in the way that she could not. Whenever we looked at my baby book there was a card taped to the first page which read, "You weren't expected, you were selected." It's the same card that my preteen daughters found looking through old photo albums under an end table that gave them a glimpse into a portion of my life that I had not yet revealed. The album was never hidden from them, but for years they never touched the ratty, beaten up pale-yellow photo album. Instead, they gravitated towards the newer, shinier ones that they were in.

One afternoon, my daughters decided to crack it open. My daughter Traci actually thought I did not know that I was adopted. From that point going forward, my adoption was open for discussion with them. I just warned them that they could not start quizzing their grandparents with 50 questions about how I came into their lives. They backed off for a few days and then their first question later in the week became everyone's favorite question - Why did Grandma and Poppop adopt? My response remains the same to this day - "Someone couldn't have a child."

My parents always encouraged me to search for my birth parents. I knew I would do so one day because I've always desired to locate them and my extended family. Regardless of my accomplishments in school, at church, and in the arts, I always felt out of place or different, but just never talked about it. Growing up, I convinced myself that being adopted didn't bother me because I had such a great family. But the reality of it is that having great parents does erase the fact my birth parents gave me up, *so how in the world could I be good for anyone else?* These types of negative questions constantly seeped into my thoughts. Feeling "less than" impacted my actions and life choices in determining what I needed to accept and deal with because I actually started to believe that I just wasn't good enough.

I want to become better at living in my truth and learning how to deal with my new family. Over the years, I endured the remarks from strangers and friends who commented to my face or behind my back that I did not look like either of my parents. Then, to make my "different" situation stand out more, there were family members who felt they couldn't chastise me like they did my cousins when they were getting spankings because "I was special." I never told my mom about those types of comments. I don't remember what we did to warrant spankings, but I remember how glad I was to be "special."

In 2013, while on an overnight college visit for my daughter Traci, I was in my hotel room pondering what I would do with my free time as my empty nest was on the near horizon. Overlooking the beautiful mountains in Pennsylvania, a TV commercial for 23andme came through loud and clear. It was a God moment. I ordered the DNA kit and waited for months for my results. While I was pleased to finally have some medical history, but the relatives I matched with were white, and I was convinced that I was Black based on what I saw in the mirror. At a work event, two years later, I overheard a colleague speak of her family's success with Ancestry.com.

In 2015, I ordered my kit. I found two matches for relatives, but when I contacted them and mentioned adoption, there were crickets. I was discouraged but not defeated. In June of 2016, I sent a message to my second cousin Pat who was literally a godsend. Pat had completed a family tree with over 2,000 relatives and was eager to help me find out how we were related. After several months, we kept coming up with deads end because we were only searching for my birth mother. On Jan 8, 2017, my cousin Pat sent me a New Year's text and asked, "Any news yet?" I didn't realize we were so far into January.

I ran downstairs to read the article about the legislation announcement event on January 9th at the State House. I didn't have a clue about what was going to happen at the State House, but I felt like I had to be there. The article led me to the website of NJCARE and the email of Pam Hasegawa from whom I learned that there was room to attend the luncheon. Fortunately, I worked an all day Saturday event and earned some time. I sent my boss a late night text informing him that, 'The laws for adoptees are changing and a big announcement is being made at the State House and I have to be there."

When I arrived there was snow piled everywhere. The State House looked like a deserted prison. There was no movement on the outside. I sat in my car for about 25 minutes as I literally couldn't move to go inside. I finally stepped out and walked into the building. It took me a short while to find the right room. The Senate Conference Room looked very small that day because it was jammed with people. All I could see were people's backs and cameras. I slowly made my way from the door to the back room where an employee who was just passing through walked out and I squeezed in the doorway. I found myself surrounded by a diverse group of people. Up front, I recognized Pam from NJCARE website and newspaper articles I had read. Then I noticed a man and a woman step to the microphone.

After an overview of the legislation, questions were asked. During the closing, the two who spoke on behalf of the group received a brown envelope. After holding it for a while they were asked if they wanted to open it in front of everyone. Both were hesitant. One of the advocates reminded the camera crew that there still was a chance that there was no new information and the birth parents may have redacted their information. The reporters then asked about their feelings knowing their information might not be there. One of the two people decided to wait until he got home to look at the contents of the envelope. The other opened hers and she only said there was a name.

As a group of strangers, we gathered in the halls and then made our way across a wide lawn behind the State House to the hotel near-by for lunch. Pam originally told me that I could attend but that I might need to bring my own lunch as all seats were accounted for. I didn't care, I just wanted to be there. I wanted to be present and in the number. The luncheon was eye-opening. I learned about the work the advocates put in to make this legislation happen. I cried through the whole thing. Dr. Stacey Patton, an American journalist, writer, author, and college professor was the keynote speaker.

Dr. Patton's story spoke volumes for adoptees. She said all the things that I could never put into words and more. At that moment my emotions took over and the tears overflowed. It was the first oppor-tunity I'd ever had to be in a room full of adopted folks, birth parents, and adoptive parents. All of them were at a point where they could talk about their adoption story without crying. To hear four of five people at a table say they felt different than the cousins and relatives in their adopted family was mind-blowing. To hear the adoptees mention how people automatically equate our search as a lack of appreciation for your adoptive parents was validated. The conversation at the table was unlike anything in my forty-six years of living that I had ever taken part in. But I know through this journey, one day the tears will fall less and the joy will come in the morning when I can share my journey with others and let them know this is all a part of one's adoption story and the overflow of emotions is a part of the adoption experience.

After the luncheon, my lifelong quest began to play out rather quickly. Had it not been for my birth mother's name on my OBC, my cousin Pat and I never would have been able to connect the dots. Thank you, Governor Christie, Senator Joseph Vitale and Senator

Diane Allen, former Assemblywoman Sheila Oliver, and countless others for their tireless efforts supporting this legislation. Many national organizations supported the bill as well, including the Child Welfare League of America, the American Academy of Pediatrics, North American Council for Adoptable Children, American Adoption Congress, Evan B Donaldson Adoption Institute and more. Their endorsements encouraged NJCARE advocates who dedicated years of their lives to the passage and implementation of this law. NJCARE members gave precious time and resources to support this grassroots effort for people like me who didn't know the magnitude of the battle they were up against. Those folks made it possible for me to now have joy *every* morning. I never qualified for the state's registry because my birth mom used the state agency, my adoptive parents used a private agency, which meant there was no overlap of records. Their decision to go a different route meant that I was not eligible to be placed on the NJ Adoption Registry that stated I was open to a reunion.

On January 11, 2017, I received a copy of my original birth certificate. I informed Cousin Pat and we finally had a breakthrough. Cousin Pat could not find Flo on her family tree. It turns out that Pat is my birth father's first cousin! We had been searching for my birth mother and we were related on my birth father's side.

Two weeks later, on January 29, 2017, I made contact with my birth mother Flo. After that day, we communicated on a regular basis via text and Facebook messages. She did not want to hear my voice and insisted that when we met on Sunday, February 12th, when she was going to give her testimony before the church, that would be the first time we both heard each other's voices in person. With my birth father, it was quite the opposite. From the beginning, all of my communication with him has been on the phone. He wanted to wait until July to meet at his wife's family reunion, but his siblings and family said no way! So he came to New Jersey in early March to meet my family and me.

There are days I feel like I can't breathe, days I feel like I want to cry but I can't, days where I'm afraid of the what ifs, and days people who don't get it can make me feel like I am doing something wrong because of my desire to search. It bothers me that I can't always find the right words to help others get it. NJCARE has provided me with resources to help me better explain.

To add to my anxiety, my therapist passed away right before I was to meet my birth mother, Flo. He had helped me sort out so many things and then he was not here to witness the aftermath of the re-union. I needed to speak to someone who was non-judgmental before I came face to face with Flo. I found another person and I was so anxious for my appointment that I showed up a day early. I selected her because she went to Hampton University, the same college my birth parents attended. There was something about her bio that resonated with me.

I had my reunion with Flo all planned: therapist on Wednesday, NJCARE support group on Saturday, February 11th and meet Flo for the first time on Sunday, February 12th. Although I wouldn't have the time to process it all, I knew after meeting that group of people at the luncheon in January they were the ones who could help prepare me for what was going to happen on February 12th. Early on, I didn't know much about NJCARE, but it was my desire to get to a better place and I thought they would be the right group of folks to help me. My goal was to one day be like them; open and passionate about the work of the adoption advocates, and be able to tell my story in a cool, calm, and collected manner.

This journey has truly been a whirlwind. My boss and my secretary have been amazing and checking in every now and then to make sure I stay focused at work. My parents are just amazing people and have been supporting me along this journey from the beginning. My three grown daughters are at various stages with understanding the magnitude of my new-found identity. They often say, "Mommy, this is *your* thing!" How can they not see that this is relevant to them? They just don't get it now, but I know they will when they are older.

Now that I know the truth, I am happier. I am whole. I will be forever grateful to Pam Hasegawa of NJCARE and my cousin Pat for their role in helping me connect the dots to my birthright. Thoughts and visuals of the reunion with my biological parents still give me goosebumps and it is difficult to contain my emotions. Every interaction with my birth parents sheds light into my being. I'm so glad that I never gave up, even when a reunion seemed impossible. This journey has indeed been a whirlwind, yet the light at the end of the tunnel has made it all worthwhile. I am proud to be adopted. I am honored to serve as an advocate for adoptee rights. Whatever the NJCARE team need me to do, I will be on hand. Some mornings I wake up and wonder if this has all been a dream. Thankfully, it's real. My circle is complete. I have found my joy in the morning, in the noonday and in the evening, and there's nothing anyone can *ever* do to take it away from me!

LESSON ONE

THE JOY OF LEARNING

1

The "A" Word

When I was old enough to read the words on the pale yellow, polyester, photo album, *"You Were Not Expected, You Were Selected,"* I thought, *What does that mean? Selected? By who? From where?* I opened the book as I had done so many times before. Still feeling the giddiness looking at pictures of me from infancy to five or six years old. In elementary school, I talked about the book and photos regularly. In some of the photos, I actually recalled those moments and recognized the surroundings, while others were totally unfamiliar. I was never the type of child afraid to speak up, and for some reason, my curiosity of this weighted, puffy, yellow photo album got the best of me. There was a card taped to the inside that had the stats from my birth: Joi Renee Fisher, 5lbs, 8 oz. It did not mention the hospital that I was born in and only listed the location of Trenton, New Jersey.

"Mommy, what does this word mean?" I asked in a startled tone, pointing at the word "Selected."

"What? Why are you pointing that out now? You've looked at that book lots of times."

"I know, but I'm not sure I like that word. It just doesn't seem right. Is there something wrong with me?"

"No Joi. There's nothing wrong with you. You're a smart girl, a beautiful girl and nothing gets past you."

"So what does it mean?"

"Well baby, like we have talked about before, "Selected" means that you are very special and chosen just for us. Your father and I wanted a baby girl so badly and we could not have one. There was a young

3

woman who gave birth to you and loved you very much. But she realized that she was too young to take care of you and wanted you to be raised by a loving family. We were blessed to adopt you. Having you in our life has been the best thing we have ever done together."

"OK, I know you've said that I was adopted lots of times, but where are my *real* parents? How did you get me? I had several more questions before she chimed in.

"Joi, your father and I went to a private agency here in town. We filled out some papers and told them exactly the kind of daughter we wanted, and they helped us get you. We were very lucky!"

My mother's calming, yet authoritative voice, let me know that the conversation was over. At least for now.

After a few moments of silence, I opened the album again and began looking at the photos. Up until that day, I never suspected that I was not a full-blooded Fisher even though I had heard the words "adopted" lots of times. I was too young to feel any type of impact of another woman out there being my mother or another man being my father. So far, the Fishers were great parents in my eyes. Over the years, the subject came up now and then, because I have a cousin who was also adopted, but it was never really the focus of family attention.

My parents had been trying to have a child for at least five years. My mother got tested and there were issues with her tubes which prevented her from conceiving. She told my dad that she did not want to spend the rest of her life without children. My dad was hesitant about adopting at first. Mom was adamant. She cornered him with an ultimatum. "Either we adopt or I'm leaving," she said firmly. They were living in Plainfield, New Jersey and she had seen a small office building with a black and white sign bearing the words, "Adoption Agency." Mom had wanted to stop in and inquire about adoptions in the past but did not have the buy-in that she needed. Now, she was ready and my dad was on board. She had spoken to both sides of the family of her intention to adopt.

In February of 1969, she made a trip to the Adoption Agency, the United Family and Children's Society. She spoke to a woman at the front desk and asked about the agency's adoption procedures as a resident of the area. At first, the woman was startled by her request. Then she proceeded to tell my mother that they only dealt with "Prime Babies" - those with blonde hair and blue eyes. She stated that my mother should visit the East Orange office as they might be able to help her. Mom left Plainfield and headed to East Orange. She walked in the door and inquired about the adoption process. The first thing the woman at the desk asked her was whether she had visited other agencies. She told them that she went to their office in Plainfield near her home and was told that she should go to this location in East Orange.

By now, the staff in the back were moving toward the front murmuring among themselves. One woman spoke up and told my mother to go back to Plainfield and they would work with her. Mom went back to Plainfield the next morning and this time the receptionist and other office personnel treated her like a VIP. They took her completed application and told her she would hear from them as soon as there was a baby girl available. After a year my parents were not sure if they would receive a baby. Then they received word of my birth in April and on June 19, 1970, I was placed in the home of my parents, Jerlene and James, at two months old after being in foster care. My mother remembers the little green dress I wore when she first saw me and was surprised by my clean face and hair. I guess she assumed that I would be dirty coming from the foster care system. I had a small brown vinyl bag with my belongings: a few diapers, a pacifier and sleeper pajamas.

The agency told my mom that she could keep my name, Sherry Lynne, or she could change it. All along, mom wanted to name me "Joy." She said that I was going to be her Joy. Then my dad's younger brother Harold suggested that she spell it "Joi" and she liked it, so that's how I became "Joi." My dad's middle initial is "R," which led my mom to select the name "Renee" as my middle name so that I could have the same initials as my dad, "JRF." The same weekend that I became baby Joi Renee Fisher, my parents took me to meet the Fisher family in Williamsport, Pennsylvania. I've been told there was a welcoming celebration in my honor.

2

The Ties That Bind

I attended Emerson Elementary School which was directly across the street from my house. I remember the stories my mom loved to repeat about my childhood. My cousin, Shawn, lived with us for a while in elementary school. I'm not quite sure how he ended up at our house, but we went to kindergarten together. We were both excited and scared because it was time for our first day of school. My mom walked us to school that morning. Shawn and I were holding hands. Mom introduced us to the crossing guard. The two of them talked for a while as we waited for the morning traffic to pass. All of the crossing guards knew the parents within the two block radius of the school. There was always someone rushing their kids to school at the last minute, flying down the street. The guard made sure she gave the reckless parent a warning.

Our crossing guard didn't play. She reminded us kids, that we had to follow the rules or she'd tell our babysitter, our momma, or she'd tell your friends momma who she was sure knew your momma. "Y'all kids are gonna listen!..." "Don't let me have to tell..." and she would always say the name of your friend or relative. Act up if you wanted to and somebody would let your parents know.

I clearly remember coming home one day and being very upset. I don't know what day of school it was, but we had a project in class to draw and talk about what we wanted to be when we grow up. I wanted to be a boy and Shawn wanted to be a fire engine. We both were upset because the teacher had the nerve to tell both of us that we couldn't be that. No explanation! I couldn't wait to tell my mom what the teacher told us. "What do you mean I can't be a boy!!" When my mom came to pick us up, she had a private conversation with our teacher.

Now I don't know what took place during that conversation, but I definitely told my mom that the teacher said I couldn't be a boy when I grew up. Mom kept saying, "Joi, we will talk about it when we get home." I'm not sure when the talk happened, but I do recall how my mom taught me everything with a book. She would always answer my easy question straight to my face, but she was more likely to answer tough questions with a book in hand.

She showed me a book about boys and girls. It was a hardcover blue book. There were photos of naked kids and I remember thinking this is just nasty. *What's wrong with her?* Then she began to explain the different body parts and how boys have a penis and girls a vagina. My mom was no-nonsense and she wanted me to learn the facts as early as possible. I don't ever recall being taught the "kiddie version" of the human body parts. She taught me what the images and the words in the book meant. I still didn't get it, but then I knew that between our legs in the photos, that boys and girls had something drastically different. I thought maybe mine would go away and transform over time. Eventually, it stuck and I realized that I could not be a boy and my dream was crushed.

What's ironic is that after meeting my birth mom Flo, I learned that she had also been a tomboy. She loved to run, jump, bounce and pounce all over things. If it was rough and girls weren't supposed to do it, she was first in line. On my 48th birthday I listened as she told this story and all I could do was shake my head. I didn't utter a word. This was yet another life coincidence. When she shared stories of running and playing with the boys, my thoughts immediately went to another one of my mom's favorite stories about me playing tag football with the boys before school every day. It just so happened to be the day after a heavy rain. A heavy rain didn't stop us. We knew at the school entryway there was a giant mat bearing the school name and everyone just lined up to wipe the mud off their shoes until they were clean enough to walk inside.

My mom recalled hearing voices outside at our front door one day when she was headed to work. When she opened the door, there stood a group of boys saying that they had an accident that morning. I stepped out from the middle of the group covered in mud from head to toe. My friend Ulysses tackled me because he was mad that I was about to beat him and almost had a touchdown. Bam! Before I knew it, I was hit unexpectedly from behind and sliding through the mud. Ulysses did all the talking at the door. I had already told them that my mom was heading to work and she was gonna kill me. I was literally covered head to toe, all in my hair and everywhere. When my mom saw me her mouth just dropped. She stood there in her pristine white nurse's uniform speechless. Ulysses kept talking. By that point, we had tried to wipe some of the mud off and just smeared it even more so into the fibers of my clothes and into my hair. She stood still, she looked at me, shook her head, and listened. She thanked the boys for bringing me to the house. She told them I'd be late for school, so they could tell the teacher. She advised them to head back across the street so they would be on time. They said goodbye and left.

Of course, my mom did not want to touch me wearing her white uniform. She was pinching my shoulder to guide me upstairs, making sure I didn't touch the walls on my way to the bathroom. We had such a high staircase, and on that day it seemed like we'd never get to the top. It was like she didn't want me to get to the top too quickly but she also didn't want me dripping and moving too slowly. I know we didn't laugh about that at the moment, but later it became one of those stories she told people.

I guess since I could not grow up to be a boy, I was just gonna be a tomboy and run with the guys. My football story is running through my mind as Momma Flo is talking, but I never brought it up. I just sat there. On one hand, I don't know if she wants to hear stories like that or if she doesn't want to know about my upbringing. I don't know what subjects hurt for her to hear me talk about since she was not a part of it all. Who knows? Maybe she would have a warming feeling hearing that my life experiences are so similar to hers.

"Knowing that I was adopted was a weird, uncomfortable and embarrassing weight that I carried. Understanding why I felt like an outcast on the inside and outside was incomprehensible, until I met my birth mother."

In elementary school, conversations about my parents began to surface. I always felt different from my classmates when I was in the third and fourth grade. I recall how no one looked like me, talked like me or had any of my mannerisms. I spent so much time defending my parents that it was exhausting. Kids were always asking, "How is that your dad? You don't look like him!" My response was the same, "That's my dad and everybody does not look like their dad!" The only problem was that everyone around me was either the spitting image of one of their parents or at least resembled them.

I don't think people realize that in elementary school, the word "parent" or "parents" comes up often in the classroom setting. This opened the door to a barrage of questions about my parents' physical features before, during and after class. Actually, in middle school, it came up quite often as well. I worked with my dad in the summer camp. I was a counselor for the younger grades while he taught middle school. My father was big on bringing in articles and discussing current events. One day while I was in my class I could hear him talking about a recent article on adoption. He told the class that I was adopted. I was shocked and taken aback. *Why did he have to tell my peers? Didn't he think about how it would affect me?* Like clockwork, after class kids came up to me and said, "Oh I hear you're adopted." "Yes, I am," I replied, trying not to make eye contact. I never told him how it made me feel uncomfortable, and that it really caught me off guard.

There were also times in middle school where I visited his kids' basketball games. I could hear people in their own joking way utter things like, "She must look like her mother!" Sometimes he would tell someone that I was adopted and other times he would agree that I look like my mother. Even though we don't talk about it, his responses bothered me. How was I supposed to feel when he says the adopted word to some people and not others? Inconsistencies like this left me wondering if he was unhappy about adopting me and not having his own child. I did not know if he was embarrassed or if I had the right to ask.

What I do know is that some days it made me angry that people even commented that I must look like my mother. I wasn't sure if they were being rude or why they felt they needed to say something so hurtful to a child. I honestly could not understand why adults kept pointing out the differences in our features. It was tough to grin and smile at the ridiculous comments grown people made to my face.

As I was looking at my pigeon-toed granddaughter strutting around the house one day, I told my daughter Jasmin to get ready for years of dance lessons. I explained to her that my mom put me in dance as a corrective action for being pigeon-toed. I still have to be very cautious of boots and sneakers that I wear because they can be dangerous. Boots tend to be the worst. If they are too heavy, my feet will most definitely be turned in as I walk. I try to be cognizant of this fact when I wear boots around my students. I've been around kids for over 20 years and they definitely will say the darndest things. I can just imagine them talking about my feet turning in as I walked down the halls.

My mom is bow-legged. She always had a cool walk even though she looked like she was riding a horse. One day we were in the kitchen mom and I explained what "bow-legged" meant. My daughter Traci chimed in and said, "No mom, you're knock-kneed!" I just laughed and said, "Your daddy was knock-kneed, not me!" "Oh no, that's you!" she pointed.

"Do you even know what it means to be knock-kneed?" I asked. Long pause. "Exactly! I am not knock-kneed. I am pigeon-toed along with your little niece."

Now my mom chimed in to reiterate, "*I'm* bow-legged!"

Traci shouted, "NO you are *not*, Grandma!"

"How are you gonna tell her what she is and isn't?" I questioned her with laughter in my voice as I shook my head.

Mom stepped away from the counter and Traci stood behind her. Mom lost a lot of weight after chemotherapy and her legs have really slimmed down. All I heard was, "WHOA. OHHHH OK! Bowlegged!" Traci admitted.

"So again, I'm pigeon-toed and my feet turn in, that's why Grandma put me in dance class at age 4."

Mom chimed in, "The doctor told me that your mother walked that way because she wanted to, and when she was ready she would walk straight, but she highly advised me to put her in dance classes."

Fast forward, to April 5th, 2018, during my 48th birthday dinner, Momma Flo shared that her parents put her in dance because she walked like a horse. It was a gallop instead of a step. As she told this story, I thought of the pigeon-toed story my mom loved to tell about me. I also thought of my youngest daughter, Tasha, who ran so awkwardly that we gave her run its own special sound, "Doo Doot Doo Doo." She bopped straight up and down and moved her arms like she was turning a double Dutch rope. I had never seen anything like that. Both of her parents are athletes and her dad and I would look at one another and say "She got that from you!" You have to see all those movements at the same time. Tasha running always made us laugh and shake our heads. So when Momma Flo talked about her gallop, Tasha immediately came to mind. I always thought to myself, *Who in the world has she seen run like that?*

At first, we thought Tasha was trying to be cute. Then we realized she just can't run! We were wrong. Turns out she is fast as hell. At the Vertical Adventures Summer Camp, Olympic sprinter and bronze medalist Thomas Jefferson eventually tied down one or two of Tasha's arms during workouts to force her to use her arms properly. So it became, "Run correctly or get one of them strapped down." The next track season she was running her personal best times. So, Doo Doot Doo Doo shines honest in the gene pool as well. I'm learning through this journey that these idiosyncrasies are not random and all of this mess is genetic.

Not only was my birth mom, Momma Flo, tomboyish like me at a young age, she eventually found her way into the world of the arts. She danced from age 6 - 60+ until she suffered a knee injury. If you want to make a sister mad, don't talk to her about that knee injury. When she talks about her love of dance, she constantly reflects on all that she can't do because of this injury. If she does too much walking her knee is guaranteed to be swollen for a few days. In the winter months, it's the worst because she is such an on-the-go person. Her knee injury has slowed her to a pace that makes her uncomfortable. When first I met her, I realized that she wasn't as old as she initially appeared. Instead, it was the cane and the limp walk from the injury that aged her.

I remember attending my first dance school for ballet. We wore black body suits, pink dance shoes, and pink tights. The class was on the second floor and there was a long set of stairs to get inside. There was always a crowd near the entrance as parents helped their kids get dressed before and after class. I was excited about my first recital because I got my hair pulled up in a bun and it was my first time wearing makeup. Playing in my mom's makeup was a no-no and she always told me that putting on lipstick was for grown people. So to be able to do all that in one day *and* dance was a real treat.

My first recital was also the last time I ever danced at that dance studio. I did not understand it then, but my clothes and other people's clothing was stolen from the room. When my friends and I came out of class, we had nothing to change into. My mom had enough. "This is absolutely ridiculous," she complained when she arrived to pick me up.

The following year I found myself at Modern Academy of Fine Arts, on the other side of the train tracks, if you will. I had gone from a school of dance where everyone looked like me to one where no one looked like me. It was a bit of a culture shock like the way I felt when I was in late elementary school. Not only did no one *look* like me. No one *talked* like me. Worse off, no one liked the same music as me. Yet in this eye-opening environment, I was surrounded by girls who could dance and they took dance very seriously. I loved to dance, but I was always in trouble because I could not remember the routines to save my life. They just would not stick in my mind. Fortunately, by middle school and high school, I had a good skill set in tap, ballet, and modern jazz. But the routines still failed to stick in my memory bank.

My memory challenges really came to my attention after a middle school basketball game. It was halftime. We were at an away game and my friends Debbie and Aleta were in the bathroom stall next to me, and Debbie proceeded to announce to everyone in the bathroom how long I peed. "Damn, what did you drink Joi?" She began to talk about a few things that happened in the last quarter. Although it had just happened, I couldn't pinpoint what she and Aleta were talking about. We'd just had a series of amazing plays and passes and increased our score to take the lead at halftime, but I didn't remember any details of what happened. Debbie and Aleta knew the play-by-play and talked details as if they were sports announcers. At that point, I knew something was wrong with my mind. Yet how do you explain that to someone? Should I say, "Sorry guys, I'm having memory issues at age 12?" That basketball situation sticks out clearly because it was a pivotal moment in my not being able to zone in on what they were talking about after I was fully present in the same moment less than five minutes ago. *Oh God, something is definitely wrong with me*, I thought.

Basketball Jones

My father, Uncle Curtis, and cousin loved to play basketball. They would meet up in our backyard and play intense games as if there was real money on the line. At the end of the games, they would leave bruised and bloodied after fouling the heck out of each other. I had no problem shooting around them, but I wasn't going to play with them.

There was only one girl on our block that played with the boys because she could throw an elbow and push just like they did.

I played middle school basketball and really enjoyed it. In the 7th grade, my team had the opportunity to run a game against high school girls. I think the purpose was to inspire us to want to play better and realize that one day we could play like them. Yet after working with the coach and getting boxed out by those big "woman-girls," there was no way my skinny bones was going to take those licks playing high school ball. Yes, I was one of the tallest girls on the middle school team, but running the timed suicides and wind sprints that the coach made us run that day were enough for me to know that I was not going to make it through high school practices. Besides, my teammates were always teasing me for being in ballet and jumping or leaping down the court.

Later that day we watched the high school girls practice in our gym. The eighth-grade girls were excited. I said loudly, "Oh no. I'm not ready for that!" So while the coach thought this birds-eye lesson was inspirational, it was intimidating. I convinced myself in the 7th grade that I was *not* going to try out for high school basketball. Coaches kept trying to convince me to try out as the season started but my mind was made up, "absolutely not!"

I am amazed at how with each passing day I learn something about myself that is directly attributed to my birth mom, Flo. She doesn't like to talk on the phone. So one day I left her a message and mentioned my short term memory. When she got back to me, I wasn't sure if I heard her right, so I asked her to repeat herself. I literally fell off my chair. To hear her say that she has *always* had a problem remembering certain types of information left an empty feeling in my gut. From middle school onward, I knew something was wrong with my memory, but I had never shared that with anyone. I just figured I forgot things and had a bad memory. I struggled with this for years and people would always say "Joi that's just ridiculous, how could you forget….?" "My ex-husband Gary would get furious with me because something would happen and he'd ask me to recall that moment... and I could not. He'd ask me to remember a certain event and I vaguely remembered details. He used to think I was joking but soon realized that I really didn't remember.

Nevertheless, as Momma Flo was talking, that empty feeling sat in my gut like the tomboy story. *Do I say something or do I leave it alone?.* This is unbelievable. After all these years and there really is something genetic going on with my memory that I was never able to describe to people. I still could not believe she was saying this. I felt even sicker. For years I was told I that I was too young to be so forgetful. As time went by and I matured, I knew that fast-paced environments and too much multitasking didn't help with my memory. I learned that if there were things that needed to be done or recalled later, I had to write them down. I write down every damn thing! I've learned to categorize and classify my files with keywords so I always know where to go back and find notes on a specific topic. The connection between the brain and the act of writing is something that I learned about later in life as an educator. This process and connection have improved my retention of information. So to hear in my late 40's that this isn't something I'm imagining and that it's genetically linked totally stunned me. I really was speechless. I eventually got around to casually mentioning to Flo that I had a similar memory issue.

Now it all makes sense. Tomboy, love of the arts, and a bad memory. Each encounter with Momma Flo revealed that I'm more normal than I ever thought. It's just that I was comparing my *normal* to those around me which had nothing to do with my genetically predisposed *normal* nature.

3

Spitting Image

During my freshman year of high school, there was a large art exhibit in the library. As I was changing classes I was approached by Dave, the security guard. He asked me if I was in one of the pictures on display in the library. A short while later, another security guard, Mills, asked me if that was me in the picture with the tiger. I think they knew I modeled, so there was a chance that it could be me, even though I knew it wasn't. I was afraid to speak up. Especially since I did not see the photo. Throughout the day, everyone came up to me and described the photo. They said I was in African garb and photographed with a tiger. During lunch, I received a lot of compliments about my picture. This was becoming eerie. As an adoptee, I longed to find people who looked like me. Yet whenever someone told me they saw someone who was my spitting image, I got this sick and panicked feeling in the pit of my stomach. I knew there was no way I was going to come face-to-face with my twin.

Midway during lunch, security guard Dave asked me if I went upstairs to see the picture. He didn't know if certain classes were assigned to go in, so he said, "I'll give you a pass to go up since you are in lunch." It was a long, slow stroll to the library. When I walked in I saw huge panels of photos of different sizes. From the door, I wondered how in the world was I going to find that one picture in the midst of what appeared to be hundreds of pictures. Our librarians had a way of setting up these displays as if we were in a true art gallery. The displays were further in the back of the room. Students were walking in and out of the room. Two more people told me they liked my picture as they were exiting the display area. I told them I hadn't seen it yet and asked them to tell me which section I could find it. They pointed me to the outside right portion of the display.

The knots in my stomach began to tighten. I couldn't just walk directly over to it, as that would be too obvious. I walked towards the middle of the display and started with the inside section of the panel the girls told me about. I decided to take a deep breath and walk to that front panel. Each picture was professionally framed and connected onto the gray wire stand. The pictures were displayed as high as above my head and went down as low as my ankle. I scanned from the top to the bottom and when I found the photograph of the tiger and my twin, all I could do was stare at it. I had never before seen someone who *really* looked like me. At that moment, to see someone that *I* actually thought looked like me was startling. There were a lot of people in the library and the area was cramped. I was frozen. Someone bumped into me with his or her book bag and then I realized I had been standing there for quite some time. I noticed there were labels on the photograph, but I didn't want people to see me staring at it too long or writing anything down.

The bell rang, so lunch was over and I went to class. After the initial shock, it hit me that I needed to go back to get the information on that picture. I returned to the library after school was over. The room was empty. Hundreds of pictures and the wire display racks were gone. The librarian was at lunch and the librarian's assistant said they packed up the exhibit before the day was over. I soon learned that after the display has been at one school, they quickly pack up and move on to another one. I was crushed. *Why didn't I just write down the information? Who cares if other students would have seen me? Was she my sister? My cousin?* After all these years, it is an image that still flashes before me. I get annoyed with myself that I did not have the courage to ask someone about the photo or write down its information. It's hard to erase these thoughts of my wasted opportunity.

For the Love of the Game

When I got to Plainfield High School, I didn't even want to attend the freshman girls basketball games. I really loved basketball and was disappointed that I was not going to play because of the *extreme* phys-icality after my middle school experience. I waited until a few games into the season before I had the nerve to check out my first one. I was so upset after the game ended. I realized that I could play just as good as some of the other girls. It hit me that the coaches "fright tactic" of tearing the girls down was meant to inspire me, but it had the re-verse effect. I became annoyed by the end of the season knowing that I could have been playing all along. Those first preseason tryouts and practices were done to weed girls out. I saw that if you stuck with it, the coaches worked with you to improve your game. I started going to more games and peeked in on their practices.

During my visits to watch the girls practice, I noticed that most of the girls that got banged around by the big "woman-girls" got bet-ter and saw playing time on Junior Varsity (JV). So the next year, I knew that I would be too old for the Freshman team, but I believed I was good enough to make JV. I learned more about the game and got knocked around by bigger players. My asset was that I could jump and was a good rebounder. I tried out and became the sixth man in the rotation on the JV team. Although I loved basketball, my mind could never remember everything that happened after the game was over. I was never able to explain to others that most of my game was immedi-ately erased from memory. I went on to become the co-captain of the team during my senior year and was recognized for rebounding. My mom never understood why my coach thought I was good because I wasn't a shooter. She didn't see the importance of grabbing a rebound. I was happy that my dancing and jumping combination also worked well for me in basketball.

Finding my Way

My sophomore year brings to mind a memorable event that is still talked about today. Midway through the second marking period, my Spanish teacher, Ms. Amos stopped me in the hall and asked me why I was in that wing of the school so often. I told her that I had class. She looked at me a bit puzzled, but I kept walking to my afternoon class. Ms. Amos was cool and kept everyone in line. She knew I was a good student so I was confused as to why she was questioning me. The next morning when I arrived at her Spanish 2 class, she called me to her desk before I could even sit down. She said, "Joi, I went to talk to your guidance counselor." My first thought was, *why would you do that? I'm getting a B in this class so far*. I stood in front of her more confused than the day before.

She went on to say, "when I saw you over here the other day and I asked you why you were back over here, you told me that you had class. So I went over to see your guidance counselor because the only other classes over here are world language classes and I know that you are not in the bilingual classes over here."

"You are absolutely right. I have Spanish 1 in the afternoon where I am getting an A in the class. You know, if she would teach the stuff before you teach it, I just might have an A in here too!"

Ms. Amos cracked up laughing. "Joi, you cannot have Spanish 2 and Spanish 1 in the same school year." I told her that I did not schedule it that way and was following the schedule given.

Ms. Amos said that my schedule had to be changed.

"I can handle it. I probably would get a B in your class because I had to learn more basics in Spanish 1 in the afternoon." Then I raised my voice and said, "Hey Y'all told me I needed two years of language to go to college, nobody said you can't take them at the same time!" She laughed and the entire class was laughing. She told me to leave my books and go to my guidance counselor. She already had the pass written out for me.

Fast forward 20 years later, Ms. Amos invited me to a membership intake meeting for Phi Delta Kappa Sorority Inc. Epsilon Alpha Chapter event. She introduced me to members of her sorority and I heard references about the girl who was taking Spanish 2 in the morning and Spanish 1 in the afternoon in the same school year. I guess my story was priceless to her. As she spoke, I just shook my head. All of the ladies were laughing. My rationale had always been that was how they scheduled me. Since I had a B and an A, I was getting my college language requirement out of the way.

It's junior year and *The Color Purple* was out and I really wanted to sing one of the show tunes. We were rehearsing in our performing arts class and I was on the sideline singing away, not realizing Lauren, one of our class songbirds was listening. She came over and said, "Joi you can really sing. Why don't you sing more often?" Lauren, Kim, and Rosetta were always singing. It didn't matter if it was in performing arts class, the halls, or the lunch room, they belted out tunes throughout the schoo day. People were always telling them to shut up. I loved hearing them because they harmonized like true songbirds. So when Lauren said that I could sing, that was a real compliment.

Then my 6'4, 250-pound friend Orlando and I started talking about me possibly singing "Sistah" for the upcoming talent show. He would be Celie, Whoopi Goldberg's character and of course, I would be Shug. It was a great idea. Our peers thought it would be a complete shock to the student body because I had never sung in front of them. More than that, it would be hilarious seeing Orlando as Celie. It sounded like a great plan. When I got home it hit me. *Did I just agree with Orlando to try out for the talent show? What the heck was I thinking?* The thought of singing in front of the entire school kept me up all night. Orlando and I would be going up again Lauren, Kim, and Rosetta. No way! That next day I approached Orlando in class and said, "There's no way I can sing on stage. I can't do it. When we discussed it yesterday it sounded like a good idea. But then when I got home I thought the class could be setting me up to look like a fool out there. No Orlando! The gig is definitely off. Not happening!"

Instead of performing, I decided to try out for the role of emcee. I had been taking a performing arts course for a year so landing this part was definitely something I could do. I got the role. In class, we learned all aspects of a performance, including being a stagehand, costumes and prop set up, sound, lights, and even how to handle hecklers. There is always someone in the crowd at these shows who says something crazy or tears down someone's performance. So I let the first couple of hecklers comments slide. They weren't bad comments, yet they also weren't necessary. The next hecklers weren't so lucky. I took the mic off the stand, peered out into the crowd and made a clever comeback. One of them said something again, and I ripped him better than the first time. Then I heard a bunch of "OOOOOOOO!" Then there was silence. All I remember is when I came off stage, my teacher gave me a high five. There wasn't another comment for the rest of the show. Lauren and her songbird crew ultimately won first place. Like I thought in the first place, *Orlando and I didn't have a chance.*

It was the first day of my senior year. I was excited that I was able to drive myself to school in my brown mini Volkswagen station wagon. I had saved my money so I could stop at Dunkin Donuts to buy my favorite blueberry muffin. Whenever I got a ride with my best friend, after we dropped off her sister, we ended up at Dunkin Donuts. On that day, I was alone and decided to make my stop. I had given myself enough time so I was not worried about being late. I got my muffin and headed back through Cedarbrook Park. My car died. I had gas and my oil was recently changed. *What happened?* I sat in the car panicked. It was a hot day and I was sweating in my cute first day of school outfit. *Oh man, I'm gonna get in trouble for stopping at Dunkin Donuts. I'm gonna have to hear my mom say, why didn't you go straight to school?*

I knew nothing about cars. My friend Alexia's father showed her how to get under the hood and use a pencil to rig the car if it stalled out. I didn't have a clue what to do, so I just sat on the side of the road thinking. It wasn't a far walk to school, but it's really hot and I don't want to ruin my outfit. I weighed my options. I decided to walk to school. I needed to find my friends so they could go back with me to the park and push my car into the parking lot. Now, I was late for school. *Who in the world is going to believe me? That my car broke down in the park and I need a few of my friends to help me push it to the parking lot.* I went to the science wing of the building because I knew a few of my girls were in my favorite science teacher's class. I knew they would not want to help me push the car because they had on their first day of school cute outfits as well. My science teacher, Ms. Adams reminded me so much of my mom.

I tapped on the door and asked her to come into the hall. I was sweaty and out of breath. After she realized that I was okay, she listened as I spoke and just smiled. I knew she'd make a smart comment about my situation and laughed out loud. I peeked into the class to see which of my girls were there to come help me. I knew they would be pissed. Ms. Adams agreed to let us leave and instructed us to hurry back. We walked to the car and pushed it to a nearby parking lot and then walked back to school. All of us were sweaty. When we came into the room out of breath and glistening, Ms. Adams looked at us and shook her head. She added, "Glad you made it back!" Thank you, Ms. Adams, for not putting me on blast in front of the class by telling everyone that my car broke down the first day of school.

A few weeks later, I was voted Senior Class President. Our senior class funds were low and we were in dire need of raising funds for the prom. We decided to have a car wash. We went around and began asking the class officers to come to the car wash. Like past events, a lot of students signed up and when the event day arrives, no one shows up. So this time as officers, we went around to classes, club meetings, and after-school groups to remind people that signed up to attend, and emphasized that they needed to show up because the officers can't run these fundraisers alone.

The day of the fundraiser arrived. We were lined up on the side of the school waving cars in to get their car washed. We had music playing, water flying everywhere, buckets, rags, soap and the whole nine. Then an argument started with my friend Orlando because a few people on the front of the line weren't wetting the cars enough for the next crew to get the suds going. Orlando got upset and started throwing buckets of water. He didn't realize that the next customer's window was open. He wet the customer from head to toe. It was a tense moment. Thankfully, the man took it in stride and in addition to paying for his car wash, he bought iced-tea and snacks.

While in high school, my neighbor, myself and a few friends, secretly drove to New York City at least once a month on the weekend. It was some of our best hang out moments. We pitched in for gas, tolls, and parking. Then we saved money for pictures because the streets were lit up with food trucks, performers and various backdrops to take pictures. I loved taking pictures and wanted to display them all around my room, but since none of our parents knew we were in New York, hanging them up in our bedroom was not an option. So we resorted to hanging our New York pictures in our lockers or stashing them in secret compartments in our bags.

Almost every time we went, we ran close to curfew. We'd fly home down Route 22 hoping not to get pulled over so we could do it again in a few weeks. Our plan worked for the entire school year. All of us did well in school and we didn't get into trouble with our teachers or our peers. We drank Bartles & Jaymes Wine Coolers every now and then, but we handled our business and never did any dumb things like our friends. I'm not stupid. I knew what would make my mother kill me. I learned over time the extent I could go with my mom. There was no way I could come home after curfew and *not* get in trouble. I knew I could never come home drunk or smelling like weed. And I wouldn't dare walk in her house with failing grades. As long as I kept these few rules in line, I gained a great deal of freedom.

So when it was our ten-year and twenty-year class reunion and I cursed around a few classmates, and had a couple of drinks, they were like, "Joi we didn't know you drank or cursed." My response was, "You weren't supposed to know." I think social media has caused young people to think that the world needs to see *everything* you do: even the wild things. Of course, as a teen my friends and I were extra when we wanted to be, but that was only for a small circle of close friends to see. Don't get me wrong, I wasn't cursing people out, nor was I drinking a fifth of liquor, but if I wanted a wine cooler or wanted you to be clear that I could cuss you out, I'd let you know. I just didn't feel it was necessary to be like that *all* the time, and definitely not around everybody. *For what?*

To this day, I tell my young people, everybody doesn't need to know your business. Everybody doesn't need to know what you do on the weekend. Everybody doesn't need to read who you like and who you have a beef with. Social media can be damaging. I feel sorry for our young people and the mistakes they make when they post negative, unflattering videos, memes, or other content. It's as if they are tainted for life and at the mercy of anyone who wants to get them back and repost. In the days of social media as adults, we also have to limit our crazy. The difference is that most of our crazy is only etched into the minds of our friends and parents. We try to drop nuggets of wisdom on our youth and many of them look at us in the current chapter of our lives thinking we don't know what the heck we're talking about. When actually we know the game, we wrote the book, we could tell them everything they are doing wrong and explain why they keep getting caught, but that's another story. As a youth, I just want them to know that they really can't say or do anything that we haven't already done, seen or heard in one shape or form. REALLY!

If our youth understood that good grades and staying out of trouble at school is guaranteed to bring you to a whole new world of freedom. Add on top of that, if you play sports, you get to see life outside of your city's walls. There was a method behind my madness in high school and I was able to attend the college of my choice.

4

Model Behavior

Whether it was dealing with my low self-esteem, body image, finding clothes that fit, or feeling out of place, my mom had a solution for *everything*. She always found a cure or activity to get me out of my rut.

Dear Ma,

There aren't enough words to say how thankful I am to have you as my mother. Thank you for making sure every need was met. Thank you for trying to find ways to build up my low self-esteem. Thank you for making sure I knew I was loved. Thank you for instilling in me that nothing is impossible. Thank you for being my perfect match.

Love, your Joi.

"Dr." Jerlene's Cures:
Walking pigeon-toed = dance class
Walking hunched over to appear shorter = modeling
Etiquette and tom-boyish. I never knew how to get myself together =
Barbizon
Pretended I was blind so I didn't have to go across the stage in third
grade for the Halloween parade = Took me to the eye doctor
Pants always too short and too big = Store 5, 7, 9 carried sizes double
zero and zero
Big mouth, loud on the playground, likes to run, jump, and climb
trees = cheerleading
Likes to tap on things and listen to music = piano lessons
Mad I couldn't get a Jheri curl like my cousins = got a Jheri curl

(And yes, I have naturally curly hair)
Big Forehead = cut a bang layer
Big gap and baby teeth didn't fall out in high school, pull them out =
braces in college

Very tall and worried about being too skinny = Runway Modeling
I started at the Barbizon Modeling School in the 5th grade. I was one of the tallest girls in the my class from kindergarten through high school. It didn't help to be skinny as well. Unfortunately, who wants to be skinny in the days of late elementary school when people are beginning to go through puberty and develop? Not me. I believe it was Judy Blume's, character in *Are You There God? It's Me Margaret* who was always waiting to develop. Well, my train had come and gone, and I was still anxiously waiting. During that time, I found myself having two different life experiences. The first was being in an urban Black school and seeing Black girls' butts and breast galore. The second was in dance school in a neighboring town where I was one of a few Black girls. My body type fit in there because pretty much everyone was slim and not developed like me or my friends at school. People were always in awe with the length of my limbs and legs. This caused me to be at odds with whether I was happy with my body or ashamed of it.

I think I begged my mom to enroll me in Barbizon because I wanted to learn about makeup and runway modeling. We went to an information session and it was pretty expensive. I was already enrolled in dance, cheerleading and piano. I didn't think she would add anything else to my crazy schedule. My parents believed that an idle mind and idle time is a sure way to get into trouble. Unfortunately, the first teacher of our courses was so bad that they had to stop the program midway and fire the person. Then they brought us back in to start our classes over.

Here, I was again in classes with no people of color, so you can imagine what makeup lessons were like—just absolutely horrible. They didn't have *anything* in my skin tone. Back then, most companies didn't even make cosmetics for women of color. After I was finished, I'd look like a perfect Sunkist orange! While I was horrible with makeup application, I was a beast at learning the runway walk. I'd walk circles around the class and the teacher often used me as the example. I was good as long as it was just our class, but when they invited people to pop in to see how we were doing, I would revert into my shell. The instructor kept working with me and encouraging me. My classmates were also very helpful, but sometimes the nerves just took over. I could walk, be silly, play around posing, and have fun, yet the moment someone new came in the door, it was back to the shy-girl drawing board.

As I was getting over my stage fright, I still had to learn makeup application. We had tests that I had to pass. It was then that I realized even with bad makeup, I was photogenic. When our first teacher got fired, we were three-fourths of the way through our program. Yet apparently, we learned a lot of things wrong, so when the new instructor came on board we had to make some adjustments. This worked to my advantage because it gave me more time to get comfortable in my own skin. By the time the new set of classes were over, you couldn't tell me anything. I was a *real* model!

I had photos for a portfolio, I could walk the catwalk, and I finally had the confidence to embrace the purpose for my legs and forehead. I could walk in heels. I knew what colors looked good on me. I knew that my body was built for this. I still didn't know a thing about makeup. I could apply mascara and crooked eyeliner that was good enough to squeak by the makeup application test. Everything else I passed with flying colors. Barbizon grad… now What?

After graduation, I began doing every fashion show there was from Pop Warner Blue Devils fashion shows to a friends' mom modeling agency photo shoots, my uncle's business magazine photo shoots, my beautician's fashion shows, and fundraising fashion shows. Soon a bunch of my fellow models began to run into each other and by high school and college we were moving and doing shows in some of the same circles.

Then one day my mom saw a sign across the street from her job about a group recruiting and training models for a designer showcase.

She shared with me the information from Randuu Avion Model Search. I was excited to give it a try because they were paid gigs and there was travel involved. I went to the audition. When I arrived, there was nothing but tall, skinny girls in heels who were as good as hell. They embraced their body image, their weird or authentic looks, and each of them was beautiful in her own way. There were girls who had the body I once desired, who in this environment couldn't get in the designer's clothes. Luckily, I made the group. The trainer was a commentator extraordinaire Randuu Avion and he loved to say, "Pose, Pose, Pose, Pose."

The dance world and modeling pushed me to learn to love me for who I am and for who God designed me to be. Yes, the boys might not like me because I'm skinny, but this designer is going to love me because I can rock his clothes! I was still dealing with body image issues in high school. Modeling, sports, and dance increased my self-esteem, but the media and boys could tear that all down in a heartbeat. Feeling good about my body one day and insecure the next day was one thing, but my face never changed. So I was tired of constantly hearing about my complexion: "light-skinned," "yellow," "redbone," or "damn near white" depending the season. Comments about my hair from Black girls, "She don't understand black hair," "Too straight, must be all the white girl in her," "What you mixed with?" "Joi got that good hair!" "Curly out of control hair" "frizzy." My struggles were real. Then Tyra Banks came along in my teenage years and put a whole new spin on tall skinny girls with big foreheads. I kept an article in my room about her. Unfortunately, it was a tabloid article blasting her on whether she had a boob job, but I thought the other comments in the article on her were good. My mom always held on to that *Enquirer*. LOL.

Walk it Out

I learned how to be a runway model working with Randuu Avion and his team in high school and early college. I was traveling and doing shows. I auditioned for Fashion Shows Unlimited with Hazel Whitfield and Paula Kilpatrick, a mother-daughter duo that both stood less than five feet tall, but the two of them were at the top of their game as commentators and fashion show coordinators. It was Karen Wade, one of their leading models, who worked with me to learn skits, routines, special turns, tricks with our jackets, and how to make quick wardrobe changes. In this group, models had to work their way up the ladder to perform in the shows and then be selected for each scene. I watched everything Karen did. She gave you face, attitude, and her walk was fierce. To add to her qualities, she was a very nice person and strikingly beautiful.

Rehearsals were like a boot camp. They did not play. You would be cut from a scene in heartbeat. These little ladies would let you have it from the sideline. One of my greatest challenges was the intimate scenes with the guys all up in your face. I had to dance with them and do routines with lots of hands around your waist or holding hands. I think my biggest fear was if my boyfriend saw this show, I wondered how would he feel. Yes, these were paid gigs, but I still didn't know how he would react about the touching. It helped that we modeled at events where folks had to pay for tickets so whoever I was dating, more than likely was not paying to see the show. Not that it was ex-rated, but some of the scenes required very sexy acting. I kept getting cut from those scenes. The bad part was that the more scenes you were in the more you got paid, and if you were in the the opening number, you were on a different payout. Karen kept encouraging me. After my freshman year of traveling home by myself every weekend, I asked my friend Natasha who was very much into drama if she ever considered modeling. She said she would be interested. I told her we would be traveling home every weekend, but that we got paid and the shows were great and a lot of fun.

Soon Natasha became my road dog. I came home every weekend for rehearsal, to go to the club, to get some of mom's home cooking, and occasionally ride in my friend's father's Jaguar— my absolute favorite car. He was always building a car. I loved the way the gold or silver jaguar emblem sat on the hood of the car and I still think the body style is sexy. I swore one day I'd buy one from him.

While in college and moving up the ladder with Fashion Shows Unlimited, I became more comfortable on the runway and had my claim to fame with Randuu Avion's folks at a show where Michael Carter from the television show "Good Times" was the host. We were prepping for the show and the designers were sizing up each person in the room by eyeballing them. There was a funny-looking colorful outfit that they selected for one of their models but because of the short time to get a full dress rehearsal run, she never tried it on.

It's showtime! We all had our outfits and we are waiting with the designer just before the finale. Not one of the designers gave me a look during the run-through. They had already identified who they wanted. I was okay with their decision because I had been picked up by everyone else but this one designer. They had limited pieces and they kept telling this girl she had the perfect body for the final look of their set. Their stuff was interesting so I couldn't wait to see their segment. I was excited because my mom and this guy from school came down to see my show. It had been a while since I had anyone at a show since we traveled and did shows often. I was ready for this thing to be over. We just needed to do our final walk in the clothes from the last designer we modeled.

The designers began to dress their models and lo and behold the girl with the "perfect body" they were raving about couldn't get in their damn dress! Why? Because they couldn't get her *and* her boobs in! Their alterations were off for the top half of the dress. It wasn't funny, but they were in a panic as they only had a few pieces. We were all dressed in our final outfit and this was their featured piece. They began to scan the room looking at body types and who was the tallest skinniest chick in the room. All eyes were on Joi, the skinny girl who didn't get a first or second look from this designer to begin with.

I was always laid back and chilling in the cut as I waited between each scene. I did not talk to anyone like some of the other models did often. They couldn't figure out if I could "pull off" wearing and showcasing their outfit. So these joker-designers were now giving me all these tips as they were squeezing my 110-pound body into this black form-fitting mini-dress. The sleeves were a flowing taffeta of yellow, pink, and green accented with red gloves. Wearing the dress was one thing, then they added a 50-pound cape that dragged two table lengths behind me that would call for dramatic effects when I came out. It was hilarious! They carried the back of the cape halfway into the room walking behind me, but then I had to make it past the MC, Ralph Carter, to the back of the runway, onto the runway platform and keep this cape on until my cue. Then I had to wait to see what dramatic effect Randauu Avion wanted me to do as Madonna's "Vogue" blared through the sound system. Randuu called out more than 50 movements for me to perform. "Pose, Walk, Pose, Pose, Pose, Walk, Turn!" These were the days of total Voguing on the runway and Randuu didn't play. If he called it, you'd BETTER do it!

This dress was their signature piece. On cue, I dropped the cape and on my arms were puffs of various colors. Randuu was going nuts and I had no choice but to hit his poses and in-between all that, walk the full turn of the runway. It was the most amazing experience I ever had modeling. I was in a zone. It helped that I didn't know where my guy friend and my mom were in the audience. It was sick and I killed it! My adrenaline just did its thing. By the time I was exiting the stage the crowd went nuts and the designers were on the sideline going crazy. Randuu had a new level of respect for me as a model from that point forward. My mom said, "did you know he was going to do that?" My friend chimed, "Wow, I have never seen that side of you!" It's moments like that that made me realize when I'm pressured or challenged to step out of my normal laid back, quiet Joi, I can take on another fierce character and get the job done. I just wish I could more freely take on that character in everyday life.

Through one of the showcase groups, I met a photographer, Dorothy Shi. Dorothy always asked me about taking the next step in my career; yet I was broke and in college. A lot of the girls could run over to New York or already worked in New York, and went on a "go see" or audition while on a break. It was a challenge to get the funds to get to New York and miss classes. I wanted to finish my degree and knew I couldn't commit to full-time modeling or even part-time. As I got closer to my senior year in college, I thought it would be a better time. I had my headshots done and began to enter modeling other competitions as the work from Fashion Shows Unlimited was decreasing. Many groups were beginning to book the Ebony Fashion Fair and fashion shows were not the big fundraisers like they once were for many organizations.

Dorothy Shi told me about a competition with Grace Del Marco Modeling Agency. I had an appointment and met with them. It was interesting because they weren't sure which look they preferred: the look with long hair or short hair. Then it depended on which person they had to come check me out. These agencies check you from head to toe to see what portions of you are marketable from your hands for lotions, to your head for hats and wigs. Then they asked me why my clothes were so baggy. I wore jeans and t-shirts in college. They wanted me to wear fitted clothes. Fitted as in tight! I didn't have anything that met their criteria except for my track team tights.

Dorothy continued to help me during my follow-up appointment. I saved money for another photo shoot. Everything was set and her makeup artist backed out at the last minute. Dorothy did makeup, but it's not her thing. Part of the photo shoot took place outside and there was snow on the ground. My makeup wasn't the greatest, but it had to do. My outfits were layered and they looked great. Dorothy was a great coach during the photo shoot and for once I felt comfortable in front of the camera. She wanted to make the shots quick as we are taking off layers and putting more on in the snow on the streets of New York. Runway and photo shoots are very different. I know where the camera is in a photo shoot. I know when the cameraman is zooming in and out. On the runway, you just look straight ahead and have no idea where the photographers are positioned.

I was now ready to enter the competition. I went through all of the prep workshops leading up to the competition. In between entering and competing, I found out that I was pregnant with my first daughter. Not a little pregnant, a lot pregnant. I was bleeding through the first three months of my pregnancy for what I thought was my regular period. During the competition, I couldn't tell anyone that I was pregnant. We had been preparing for this event for a few months. There were big prizes on the table to help me move into this career with several photo shoots and events lined up. I was three months pregnant by the time I went to the doctor. The competition was held when I was six months pregnant.

I won the competition at six months pregnant which had a bathing suit portion. This shows how small I carried. I won the best body category which definitely was a personal joke to me. After the show, Dorothy and one of her helpers were talking to me, they noticed that I wasn't super excited. I told them that I was pregnant and was disappointed that I was not going to be able to enjoy any of the stuff that I won because events were set up for a couple of months which meant I would be in my eighth month. My dreams to become a model after winning a great contract with the agency came to a screeching halt.

The ride home from New York was a long and dreary one. The agency called me the following week to set appointments and talk about next steps. I had to reveal to them why I could not book any appointments with them in the coming months. All the highs and lows of the competition went right out the door. I had done several competitions, but this one was by far in the top. From that point on, I slid in the background. Gone were the days of runway modeling and photo shoots. All my life I've heard, "You should be a model." After repeated comments from store employees and my staff of 20+ years, I would just smile and not say anything.

Years later, I found out that my favorite store was looking for professional women at the top of their fields. They outlined the criteria and I submitted my resume, experiences, and photo to The Limited's Look of Leadership Campaign for the East Coast. The Limited sold tall pants made from good quality material. Although they were pricey, I thought I just might be able to get a discount or free clothes if I appeared in the campaign. Luckily, I was selected for this paid gig. They chose a corral suit for me to wear. That color was a leap for me because I had been wearing black, white and earth tones for decades. It was a great experience meeting women from around the country. Afterward, we were given a store credit. I purchased a black and white winter coat and several corral tops, which definitely added a great splash of color to my wardrobe.

5

Unknown

After high school, I ended up attending college in the same city where I was born— Trenton State College now called The College of New Jersey. The impact of potentially hanging out with my birth family never dawned on me. I had not applied to many schools because I didn't intend to go to college. I wanted to enter the work world and model. My mother insisted that college was not an option. She made sure we visited college campuses. When we went to Trenton State, I fell in love with the campus and that became my first choice. During my freshman year, I was so homesick even though my dad would come and pick me up for dinner. It's funny how we always received stares. I wondered if people thought he was my sugar daddy. It was important for him to take me out, get dressed up, and make sure I knew about fancy restaurants. If you did not know us, you would think our dinner date was something more than a father-daughter evening. Dad really wanted me to see how a man is supposed to treat a woman. Yet being in Trenton felt even stranger when people stared. Many older people eventually found the courage to approach me to ask my last name because I looked just like someone in the "Fitzgerald family." *Was I interacting with my real family members?* I often wondered.

I met my boyfriend Gary in college and we broke up and got back together several times. We finally got engaged during my last semester. Four months later, we were surprised to learn that I was pregnant. We were surprised because during the first three months of my pregnancy with my daughter Jasmin, I had no idea that I was pregnant. I bled monthly, leading me to believe that I was on my regular menstrual cycle. It wasn't until that third month that I bled for several extra days. Then in the fourth month, my period never came. I went to the doctor with thoughts that maybe all those extra days made up for the skipped period or that I could be pregnant.

I took the test in the back room of the doctor's office and when I came out I handed the strip to the nurse. At first glance, she looked and said that it had not registered yet. Then we read the strip together. That positive sign was as clear as day. At that point, she knew my reporting fourteen days of bleeding could mean that I had complications. She shared two options for my care. She was affiliated with Muhlenberg Hospital in my hometown and Robert Wood Johnson University Hospital in the neighboring town. As children, we always heard kids call Muhlenberg "Killinberg," because they said once people go in they don't come out. Why that ran through my mind as an adult who had been to Muhlenberg several times, I don't know, but in her office it did. I was familiar with Robert Wood Johnson's work in various medical research disciplines.

As I was familiar with Robert Wood Johnson's reputation in a variety of medical research, I informed her that I would go there. The nurse informed me that it was considered one of the best hospitals in the world for high-risk pregnancies. *High risk? Why would she use that term without going into detail?* I wondered. This is where my lack of questioning skills did not help. Since I won't ask, I'm going to use my context clues. I wasn't supposed to bleed during the early trimester of my pregnancy and I surely wasn't supposed to bleed for fourteen plus days, hence the label high risk. She asked me to make my appointment immediately. During my initial intake and visit at Robert Wood Johnson, I was repeatedly asked about my family health history. *Does anyone read the forms we fill out?* I clearly write" N/A" as my response to medical or Family History, or I write, "Adopted."

It was then that I realized how important my medical information was, but I wasn't ready to think about a search for answers. I was scared and just beginning to learn what having a high-risk pregnancy really meant. Even though a small voice inside of me wanted to find out, I was too stressed with my still-secret pregnancy to search for information. I was fresh out of college, job-seeking, and unmarried. I was the third grandchild on my paternal side to get a college degree and the second on my maternal side. I felt like I should have been an example for my little cousins instead of another unfavorable statistic. I was very disappointed in myself, but now was not the time to go on an investigative wild goose chase regarding my birth parents to find out the answers to my medical history. I was an emotional mess.

Before I knew it, Jasmin was born. At this point, she and I would be the beginning of my family health history. It sucked for her medical history as well. For months I kept that section blank until the doctor reminded me that I needed to know her father's family medical history. I did everything I could to get Gary to ask his parents about their family medical history. Since they were in another state, I hadn't developed a relationship with them. Our conversations, when we had one, was always small talk.

It's now 1995, which is two years later, and I have given birth to baby number two, my daughter Traci. The information request began again. Doctors and their assistants were not reading my note on Traci's paperwork that said "N/A" or "Adopted." The few details Gary gave me did not help establish the girls' medical history. Although it's two years later, I still didn't have enough of a relationship with his family to have a medical history conversation. He always called them and I spoke to them from his phone. I never knew their phone number. I decided it was bad enough not to have any medical history for Jasmin, but now I had two children and I needed some answers to truly establish a good medical history for both of them. I went online and began to Google ways that I could obtain my medical history as an adoptee. I didn't know the name of the agency that my parents used, but I knew it was in my hometown on Seventh Street.

I love doing online searches. I entered the words "adoption agency," "7th Street" and the city we lived in and the information popped up immediately. I began to study the website. I found the Services tab and it listed "Search" as an optional service. When I called to ask about the services I told them about my quest as a mother of two to find my medical history. They informed me that they do not release information, but that I could hire someone to assist with the search for a couple hundred dollars or I could request my non-identifying information for less than a hundred dollars. I shared with Gary the two options and decided I would invest in the non-identifying information in hopes that there was some information on my birth parents' health.

I sent my letter to the agency along with a check and requested my "non-identifying" information. I received a large yellow envelope with two sheets of paper a few weeks later. When I opened it, my eyes immediately focused on one sentence: "family was not aware of her pregnancy." I dropped the papers and cried like a baby. Those words meant that my mother wanted me to be a secret. Never to surface. Those words echoed in my head. Later in the day, after I gained my composure, I read a little more. Then I started to feel sorry for my birth mother. *I hope she wasn't raped*, I said to myself.

I continued to read, eagerly awaiting vital health information. Drumroll please: "*The extent of my health record is "Birth mother and father in good health.*" Needless to say, I was angry, disappointed, and still without answers. I contacted the agency the next day and a woman told me that the information my birth mother put down was all that was required during the '70s. She went on to say that my birth mother wrote a lot more than what most birth mothers write. So, if there is one positive take away from the whole experience, I learned that she likes to write too!

With still not much to go on, here I was in this *déjà vu* moment answering the same questions to the best of my ability on Jasmin and Traci's medical history forms. I was annoyed. Why is this doctor asking me these questions? He's holding the form with my answers right in front of him. Did he ever read the part where I wrote "Unknown" or "Adopted" or "N/A"? I was beginning to think doctors just ask these questions of adoptees to hit a nerve. For the record, once I settled on an obstetrician-gynecologist, family doctors and family pediatrician they did a great job in helping me establish my daughter's medical history. Especially after daughter number three, Tasha. It's a good thing my kids were really young and busy playing with toys when I spoke to the doctors, so they didn't hear nor understand what I meant about not knowing their medical history or about my being adopted when I explained it to the doctor.

6

Faith Walk

Now that my daughters are grown, there's been a nagging, more like yearning desire in my life to find out more about my birth parents. I thought I was okay not knowing anything beyond the little I received, but for some reason, it began to consume me. *Why was life bringing these circumstances of my past front and center now?* I asked myself. I was on a real mission. Determined not to give up. In the beginning, it felt like "Mission Impossible." Since the State of New Jersey was not forthcoming with pertinent or new information for adoptees original birth certificates.

With what I now know as my *amended* birth certificate, I at least had validity that I was born in Trenton, New Jersey. My father admittedly says he was not as involved on the front end in the adoption process and as he's gotten older his memory is not very accurate. But my mother always believed she read somewhere that my birth father was of West Indian descent or that his parents were. She remembered some comment about his complexion and hair. People look at my hair in its curly or straight state and my complexion and that becomes the opening to the conversations with strangers, *What country are you from?*

My girls think because I am lighter-skinned than they, that people get confused by my ethnicity, yet when people see my girls in the summer with their tans, they don't think of them as anything else but African-American. Their dad had what I call colorism issues. Even when visiting his family in the south there were still little comments about light-skinned people thinking they were better than dark-skinned people, which was usually followed by, *"But not you, Joi."* So my girls grew up thinking only mommy would be drawn with a yellow or orange crayon. They thought people would always know they are Black. What they didn't realize was that as children they spent a lot of time in the sun toasting them to a brown that wouldn't always be as evident as they got older and spent less time in the sun. I just sat back and waited for each of them to go off to college and come home and tell me about the dude that approached them at a party saying that they looked exotic or saying they had never seen anyone who looked quite like them. Their awakening was coming.

Years passed and I was taking Traci off to college in Pennsylvania. My separation was very fresh for me as we had a rough few months before Traci went off to college. It was during her overnight trip at Mansfield University that she stayed on campus with the team and I was alone in the hotel. It was the first time that I had nothing else to do but rest and be still. A commercial came on television and I heard the song *Getting to Know You*. The voiceover said, "Get to know how your DNA connects you to the world," and then I saw information flash across the screen about this DNA test to give you insight to your genealogy and your medical history. *Did that commercial just say I can get my medical history? Lord, in my moment of stillness you bring this up. Did that really say medical history?* I sat in the room staring off in the distance. There were big beautiful mountains outside my windows. I pondered the thought. *Lord, I know I've been praying day in and day out about what I'm going to do with another child out of the nest. I've been asking myself what am I going to do with all this extra time. Is this my answer? You send this to me now? My first moment of stillness, of peace and quiet? This would be a disruption or are you saying the time is right?*

I began to reflect on all the reasons why I couldn't do this in the past. I could not do a search in high school because I couldn't even emotionally deal with seeing a picture of someone who looked similar to me. I couldn't take hearing that a friend saw someone who looked like me in a neighboring store. I could not do a search after high school because I was going to college, and freshman year would be a headache enough. The adjustment from an urban school to a suburban college was a culture shock. I was also having meltdowns when I'd be out in the Ewing and Trenton area and people would ask me if I was related to a particular family. I'd be paralyzed with fear because I was in the city of my birth. I wasn't ready. Later, I could not do a search after college because I was engaged, pregnant, and planning a wedding. I wasn't ready because I was waist deep in triple stress.

Now here I was sending off my second daughter to college, separated, and sitting in these beautiful mountains by myself with no clue as to how I was going to fill my empty nest time. I paused and reflected on the commercial and thought there was no better time than now. I was ready. I went online to learn more about the company. I checked their reviews, I read more about the medical research and was amazed at the reports listed on the site and what they said they would be able to tell me about my medical history. I pulled out my credit card and decided to make an investment in me. *Lord, I was just planning on running to the store because I don't want to be alone in this hotel room. I don't want to sit still and let thoughts of that horrible night with Gary fill my brain. I don't want to relive that argument, the police, my Dad, the girls crying, or the fear I felt. I know if I sit still in this hotel I will break down. Lord, it has to be you telling me to take this moment and sit down.* The television was literally on for background noise. To hear that commercial in my moment of absolute peace I knew that was nothing but God and if I truly believed that, I had to be obedient and be moved to action. I almost questioned God when I saw that ninety-nine dollar price. I stopped short of questioning him and said *Lord, you do realize I'm dropping a child off at college? You know I have two in school now, you know the tuition I just paid. Ninety-nine dollars? Am I really supposed to be doing this now?* I had less than three hundred dollars in my bank account. I was a week away from payday and we needed money to get home.

I couldn't get the words "medical history" out of my mind. I opened an account with 23andme.com to begin the DNA process. My kit came fairly quickly. It was a saliva test. It required you to do the sample on an empty stomach. As a person who likes to snack, I kept forgetting that part. Trying to get the test done at night was interrupted by my snacking. I decided to do the test in the morning before I got started with my day. Once the test was mailed out, I received random emails from 23andme informing me when the kit was received, when the vials got to the lab, that the vials were being tested and the results were being processed. I was checking for updates every week. While waiting, I received an update that said 23andme was having some legal issues with providing clients medical history and that there was a pending lawsuit. Clients ordering kits after a certain date might or might not be given access to their medical history. I was furious. I purposely brought their kit because it mentioned medical history.

While waiting for 23andme, I had been researching ancestry.com. Everyone who spoke about ancestry.com for their DNA searches did mention a medical side to their reports, yet it was something ancestry didn't advertise. I needed this data from 23andme and was not ready to look elsewhere. I checked back with 23andme's website and realized the results would take months. I didn't know if the dates they were using to cut off access to the medical records impacted me. I bought my kit before the date mentioned, but I knew I wasn't going to receive my results until after the dates listed. *Lord, you sat me down long enough to find out about this company, now this? I'm praying you are going to work this out for my good.* As I read more about the lawsuit, I became more and more nervous. These medical results were so thorough that folks were finding out the illnesses they were genetically predisposed to and freaking out. I asked myself, *Joi are you ready for that? What if you read that you are predisposed to a terminal illness? Can you handle that? What are you going to do if you find out something like that?* All these thoughts were running through my head. Then a calm just overcame me. *This did not happen by accident. This is bigger than me. God brought me to this so I just have to lean on what I believe He is telling me to do. I will finally have some information about ME. If I don't get my medical history, at least I'll be able to answer "the what are you" questions. Just pray and don't worry, Joi.*

Three months later I got the email stating that my results were in. When I went to the website and logged in, there was a disclaimer and information about the lawsuit. I learned that medical information was overwhelming for many people. I had to agree to hold 23andme harmless in the event they delivered bad news. The company then required folks who purchased kits within a certain period of time to click and sign a waiver not holding them responsible for the information you were about to discover. They made several recommendations for support services in different medical fields and they stated that just because you had the genetic markers for certain diseases and illness that did not mean you definitely would or wouldn't get it. The DNA markers identified the ingredients that make up the illness. If you agreed to accept responsibility for your own mental health you signed off stating you wanted your full reports.

Upon receipt of my results, it turns out that I am more European than I imagined. In life, I had always been told that I had hair like a white girl, features and build like a white girl, but I never wanted to accept that label. My brown skin meant I was Black; end of story. As the DNA results and matches came in I did not see one Black person in my matches, nor one person of color. I couldn't believe it, not one. I checked back regularly and then I stopped checking the site.

I went back to 23andme months later and saw that new matches had hit my inbox. So many profiles did not contain a picture, but their profile let me know they were not people of color. I couldn't get mad about that because I used a black and white sketch of one of my pictures as my profile picture. I didn't want people to know my features. A few people of color listed as 4th, 5th, 6th, and 7th cousins began to surface. I began to wonder if I should try another site. I couldn't ask anyone because then someone might ask me questions that I was not ready to answer.

A few weeks later at a work gathering, my colleague shared a story about the great success her family had with tracing their family history and their experience using Ancestry.com. She and her sister were actually preparing for some sort of taping about their story and their results. I tried not to get too excited and wanted to ask so many questions, but we were there to enjoy some downtime after a hectic work week. *God, it's you again, I know. This woman is interceding on your behalf and she doesn't even know it. I hear you!* I knew I had to try the Ancestry website. The process was the same. I ordered, submitted, and I didn't check weekly. I patiently waited for that final email. Once my ancestry.com DNA was uploaded I was able to connect with a few cousins. All of these bits and pieces of information made me want to find my birth parents even more. I was beginning to see people with similar features as mine or those of my daughters. It was crazy. I did not want to say I was doing this just for my medical history. Many adoptees say that in the beginning because it is a safe way to go through the process without the ridicule from those who don't understand why you are doing it. I also think it's easier to say you only want the medical history because what if in the end your birth parent does not want to see you? Then you can say that you didn't want to see them either, and you only needed the medical information.

I am forever guarding of my personal life. Yet I am not ashamed of being adopted or wanting my medical history as it was an essential missing part when my children were younger. It is important as I'm aging, but it is only a part of my *why*. Now that 23andme provided my medical history, I was on a mission to find my family and learn more about my ethnic background. For years, I felt such a void. A huge hole of nothingness. I've always known that my relationship and friendship issues were impacted by my fear of abandonment. I fear letting people know how much they mean to me. I hang on to things that may not be good for me for fear of being alone. I often question if I am loveable or if I am good enough. Maybe I was feeling lonelier because my second child was heading off to college five hours away. Maybe it was because of my recent separation and upcoming divorce. I'm not sure, but the emptiness was weighing heavily on me. Feelings of abandonment, fear, and rejection became overpowering. Then again, it could have been the feelings of deceit, embarrassment, and disappointment surrounding the impending divorce that had me on an emotional rollercoaster.

7

Forever Family

I have several unmarried female friends that are in their 40's and not in serious relationships. Many of them are wrestling with fact that they may have waited a little too long to settle down and have a child. In doing realistic calculations, their concerns about a missed window are growing. I wish I could say that I always encourage adoption to friends but I don't. I am the first to advocate for adoption *if* the subject comes up, but I've never told people why. It was tough being a "closet adoptee." I was often flabbergasted by the ignorant comments educated people make about raising someone else's child.

Another friend adopted her daughter two years ago and that made me so proud. Even though I had nothing to do with her decision, I just know that it takes a special person to adopt a child in any of the forms of adoption occurring around the world. The highest percentages of adoptions in the Black community come from family relationships with one relative legally taking over as the child's parent or stepparent. My friend's actions as a single mom told me about her heart that I did not know, and that makes me even happier to have someone like her in my circle.

There is also another couple who adopted sisters and their journey has been fun to watch from a distance. Adoption is a difficult decision and adopting older children can be more challenging as this also takes a certain level of commitment and dedication. Watching this couple give these girls a forever family warms my heart. I couldn't tell them over the years about my experience because I didn't talk about my own adoption. One day this friend came to work and he was upset because children at his daughter's school were teasing her because she didn't look like her parents. I wanted to say something to him as I had been there more times than I could count, but I just couldn't get the words out of my mouth.

To be honest, I'm just learning to embrace being open about my adoption journey. My colleague expressed his anger about the cruelty of the children and he happened to bring his daughter back to work with him that day. I heard her telling the secretary why she was sad that afternoon. I decided to double-back when the office was clear to say to her that I knew how she felt because I was an adoptee who didn't look like my dad either. I told her about picking her battles because there are a whole lot of people in the world with natural born parents and they don't look like them either. I encouraged her to just say, "Yeah, I know we don't," and let it roll off her back.

That summer my colleague, his wife and their two daughters came to Traci's graduation party. I called the little girl and her dad over to me. I said, "Remember I told you that I was adopted and people told me I didn't look like my dad. Well, let's go meet him so you can see for yourself." I wanted her to see that I wasn't making this up for her to feel better. When I took her and her parents over to my dad, her mouth dropped open. I said, "Whether we look like our parents or not, they love us just the same. I told you about ignoring the other kids because I've been there and I know if you act like it bothers you, they will continue to tease you. I learned that if you don't make a big deal out of it, and agree that we don't look alike at all, then the joke is over and I won!"

Every time she saw me that day she smiled brighter. That was a huge moment for me. I had never shared with my dad that the two of us not looking alike was something that bothered me all my life. I couldn't let that young lady continue to think that she was the only one dealing with such an uncomfortable issue. Now my colleague 's mouth just dropped because I said everything to his daughter so matter of factly. He didn't have a clue that I was adopted and he and his wife had known me for years. It was literally a drop the mic and walk away moment. He thanked me at the end of the night and still expressed his shock. It was small, but big moments like this that let me know I was ready for more information about my adoption and to share my story with others. After the party, I created Google alerts for any news on adoption. I could also always count on my dad to place the most recent articles on adoption in my mailbox. Between my dad and my mom, a local article on adoption never got past them without making me aware of it.

8

Close Encounters

Fortunately, with ancestry.com, I was finding family members of all races. At the time, I found a second cousin. I didn't fully give up on the other website because I found a first cousin on 23andme. *You heard me right! After a few months, a first cousin and a second cousin!* Reaching out to people on these website takes a certain boldness. I wish I had my mom or Jasmin's personality. Then I could send the matter of fact type emails asking direct questions and tell them that I'm looking for answers. Adoptees know that with adoption comes family secrecy, so anyone I dropped the "A" word on, I had to realize that they may not respond to keep the peace and not expose a family secret.

In my initial emails, I started out with very brief statements to generate a back and forth dialogue. Then I dropped the "A" bomb. At first, this guy who was a 2nd or 3rd cousin on 23andme asked me a lot of questions. After dropping the word "adoption" all I heard were crickets. I was distraught. I found him on Facebook and he looked like me and my girls. Rejection again. This time it was intentional. *Why am I doing this? Why am I putting myself through more rejection?* I asked myself numerous times. After months and deep prayer, I resorted to the results on ancestry.com. I came across a woman who was my first or second cousin on ancestry.com. I could see another profile that connected her to another woman identified as her daughter. They were at the top of my matches listed in a row. I analyzed her profile and saw that she had an extensive family tree with nearly two thousand branches. *Who in the world takes the time out to map two thousand folks? It could only be someone who is interested in their family history.*

That was a plus for me. People like this usually don't care how you are related to them. They just like putting pieces of a puzzle together and the mystery of figuring things out. We all have a family member who we can say, "Poppa was a rolling stone." With two thousand branches, I can't possibly be the only surprise.

I had so much more confidence after finding this God-sent relative. My guess was that she was a problem-solver. It was unbelievable. I searched her profile for the surname I often heard when I was in college and I didn't see it. I decided to follow my own advice and reach out to her via email. *What's the worst that could happen? She could say no, but at least I would have acted. I have to stop sitting back and living with the what-ifs in life because I'm afraid to ask the tough questions. Suck it up Joi.* Her profile let me know that she was into genealogy. With three relatives this close in the blood, I can't waste any more time. I sent her one "hello" message. Then in the second email message, I didn't hesitate and went directly to adoption. I wanted to cut to the chase so I wrote something like, *if you are not interested in connecting I am okay with that. I also mentioned that I know adoptions in the '70s left someone with a scarlet letter and it's not my intention to disrupt anyone's family, but I'm searching for answers.* She insisted that I call her as soon as I could. It took me months to dial her number. I finally spoke to her and learned that she lived in the Washington, DC area, and was my cousin Pat. When she looked into the DNA of her known second cousins, we used my birth parents demographics that was outlined in the non-identifying information document. We knew we were closely related and she was amazed because the markers were so close.

I remembered that both of my birth parents were twenty-three years old when I was born. We were working from my memory because I couldn't find the paperwork. I knew I had it stashed away because I'm a pack rat, but I had not been able to put my hand on the right files. We thought our connection was through my birth mother but then Pat thought it could be my birth father. I told her about the relative on 23andme who never resurfaced after I mentioned adoption. She told me to go back and look on that site and read some of the family surnames he had listed. Later that evening I had my laptop out working from the comfort of my bedroom. We were on the phone for hours combing through various pages on the website. She agreed to purchase a 23andme kit so that her connections could be matched with his to see what we could figure out. Even though we felt like we were making headway, we knew it would take months for answers.

When I looked at her two family trees I finally saw the cousin's surname who did not respond to me, listed on her surname list. Pat continued to look at male and female relatives on her family tree of the thousands of folks she organized. Nothing seemed to match. She looked at the locations where folks were living to see if anyone was in New Jersey who was around sixty-nine years of age. I was so excited and anxious at the same time because I was beginning to get real information. My parents knew that I had done the DNA test. I shared with them my revelation while sitting up in the mountains of Pennsylvania all alone and we have had good conversations about it. As I combed through my cousin's ancestry profile, I noticed that the city she lists that she grew up in Virginia sounded very familiar. As we talked, I learned that she lives seven miles from where my father's mother grew up in Ruckersville, Virginia. *Seven miles.* That's pretty close I thought. She also had "Taylor" listed as a surname within her family. My father's mother was a Taylor. *What if my adopted father is related to me from my birth father's side of the family? Now that would be some creepy stuff!* We haven't found the link, but my cousin was determined to solve this mystery.

Cousin Pat asked if it was okay to introduce me to other relatives via social media. She said that they found several relatives over the years who were unknown due to family secrets. She reiterated that finding a new unknown relative would not be unusual. Using similarities from the cousin we found on 23andme and her information, she sent a private Facebook message to that branch of her family tree. She said "We found another cousin. We have a lot of DNA markers that match!" She gave a little bit of my back story and the welcome to the family messages began pouring in. This was absolutely crazy! Cousin Pat hasn't met me a day in her life and she was introducing me to the family and inviting me to the family gathering in a couple months in Virginia. She and I had great conversations over the year and a half, so this was absolutely mind-blowing. I literally couldn't keep still. I didn't want to stop and think. It felt like a storm was brewing around me and I was standing in the eye. If I moved to the left or to the right, I was going to be swept up into this whirlwind and lose my mind. *Cousin Pat is phenomenal! Lord, what am I supposed to do with all of this? I don't know where Pat's research is going to get us, but my bloodline to her, her mother, and her son are closer than her known second cousins. What are we missing? Why isn't this adding up? Why can't she find a match?*

I decided that maybe it's best that I look for that paperwork with my non-identifying information to make sure we were working from the right data. Having an empty nest had given me the time to do more research. I took a few days after school and combed through boxes and file cabinets. I couldn't find the document, so I decided to google the adoption agency again. I found the email address I sent the original request to and sent an email requesting another copy. I had already paid for the information back in 1995, so I was hoping they only charged me for a photocopy and not the entire document. I gave up my search for the night at almost two o'clock in the morning. *God knew what he was doing. There would have been no way I could have handled all that comes with this birth family search when I was in high school, or college, or a new mom. This is just the beginning and I am already an emotional basket case. I can't let anyone know that at any moment I may fall apart since I have a household to keep together. I have a new job. I am what keeps this family afloat.*

As I prepared for bed I walked in circles and prayed, *Lord, thank you for this day, thank you for this moment. Lord thank you for all that you've done and all that you are about to do in my life. I can't tell you that I have a clue about the journey or the direction for the next phase of my life, but I know that my moment in those mountains in Mansfield,*

Pennsylvania was the start of something new in my life. That moment was the start of a new beginning that I would have no control over. But Lord, today I stand before you because I do have control over finding this non-identifying document that I requested back in 1995. Unfortunately, you know that I am a pack rat. You know that I don't throw things away and something is lost that can't be found. I know it is here in this house. I know it is somewhere right under my fingertips. I ask that you help me remember where this paperwork might be. Lord renew my strength and my energy as this journey has just begun and it is already taking a toll on my sleeping patterns. YOU KNOW I need eight hours or more. I ask that you lead me and guide me as I continue to sort through my many files. It's a blessing that my paperwork is organized. I just need my hands on the right crate. Something important is lost Lord that I can't find. Please help me. In Jesus name, I pray. AMEN.

Getting the document again from the agency may take some time through standard mail. My plan was to rest, go to work, and try again tomorrow. I woke up absolutely exhausted, but I made it through the workday. Before I began my search that evening I asked God to guide my hands and footsteps. I decided to check this small black filing case. I kept walking by it last week, but I was sure I knew the files that was in there because I used that case regularly. Then I noticed a small gray filing case out of the corner of my eye. I began to shuffle through the paperwork. Voilà! There was a file labeled "Certificates." I found Tasha's birth certificate— we had been look-ing for that. *Thank you Lord that was an added bonus.* I turned back to the black case and flipped the lid and I saw at the front of the bin a stuffed file labeled "Joi." I flipped through quickly and nothing. Then I looked back in the file once more and there was a file labeled "Adoption." *REALY Lord! REALLY! This document was in the filing case that I kept passing by to check other bins and file cabinets be-cause I KNEW what was in there.*

BAM! There it was in black and white! I took a picture of a portion of the document and sent my birth mom's description of herself to Pat.

I explained to Pat what the adoption agency shared with me, letting Pat know that we have a lot more information to work from compared to what many birth mom's wrote during that time. At that moment, I realized that I had been working from the wrong age. My birth mom had me at 21 not 23. Therefore, Pat was looking at relatives who were 69 years old when she should really have been looking for people who were 67. With thousands of individuals on her tree, I knew that detail would make a difference. She began to search for women who would have been born in 1949.

I went through Pat's family tree again. This time I focused on the ones who had pictures. There were lots of fair-skinned Black folks. The further down the family tree some of the images were not clear, so it was difficult to tell their skin tone. Pat's search continued and she could not find a female relative who had been in the New Jersey area in the 1970s. She then asked me to send the information from my birth father's side, hoping that maybe that could be the link. She mentioned some rolling stones on various sides of her family tree and again reiterated that a new relative for some of them would not be astounding. As we looked at each other's pictures we also wondered at one point if we could be long lost, sisters? Wouldn't that be crazy!

Pat combed through her two thousand relatives on her family tree again and she told me that she would get back to me as she did more research. She always sent me updates and communicated with me along the way. At that moment, I also shared with Pat some of the updates to New Jersey's adoption legislation regarding the open birth records. I thanked her for all her work and told her that if she wasn't able to find a connection between us that it was okay because soon I could apply for my original birth certificate. I forwarded her some of the links to the articles published in the past year. I wanted Pat to know that we would soon have a name *if* my birth mom didn't redact her information. I was excited that we would have some legitimate information to work with. I explained to her how the law came about and how this would work in our favor.

New Jersey advertised the new law via television ads and reporters wrote articles informing birth parents that they must make their decision to redact their information or express any parameters they want in place for notification or reunion requests before the end of the year. They were to notify the State Department by December, 2016 because as of January 2017, that option will no longer exist. I wondered if my birth parents received the notices. *Did they send out notifications to all birth parents? Did they send out notification to adoptees? Or adopted parents? If they sent out notifications to birth parents individually the way the opposition made it sound like birth moms absolutely expected anonymity, so they don't want to be found. Do most birth moms really feel that way? Today, teen pregnancy out of wedlock on reality shows is a daily occurrence. Do these birth mom's still believe they will be judged?* I had so many unanswered questions roaming in my mind. If my birth parents chose to redact their information they were supposed to at least provide their medical history for the adoptee. Actually, since I had a ton of information from 23andme, I was not as pressed for medical history. There are a million other things I wanted to know about my birth parents and about me.

I can't say that I was happy with the laws allowing a redaction, but those against the legislation advertise that this notification will impact folks willingness to place children up for adoption. If allowing the adoption redaction option *really* means allowing more children to be given life, then I have to accept that. Well that's the way one side of the field makes it sound. I was beginning to buy into their rationale. I'd rather have birth mothers remain anonymous if that means they would give the child life. I don't think that has anything to do with our getting our records opened. The majority of today's adoptions are more flexible. Open records have not slowed the pace of adoptions. I do believe that the opening of these records for many will make the feelings of shame resurface in the lives of women who were told some very cruel things when they relinquished their children. I don't think those feelings will ever go away. There are all kinds of successful family situations that folks in the world of adoption have researched. Today, they use better strategies to deal with adoption and through open adoptions helping adoptees with their identity. Now that I was close to solid answers, I found myself flip-flopping around the issue. Most of my uncertainty on taking a solid stance had to do with the power of the media and advertising, while the lives of adoptees hung in the balance.

9

Stir up the Gift

My vocal journey has been strange. I had grown up singing alto in the choir at Plainfield High School, but at times I had difficulty singing those lower alto notes. I didn't want to move to the soprano section because all of my friends were altos and there were at least "fifty-thousand" sopranos. Everyone wanted to be a soprano. Of course, half of them didn't belong there, but that was their choice. We had a new music teacher so she was just learning our names, faces, and sound. She allowed us to stand wherever we felt comfortable.

College was a different story. Trenton State College (TSC) had a great gospel choir. I was so excited to join, but terrified as well. I stressed over whether I had to audition to sing or whether I would be automatically welcomed in with open arms. I figured that in college they expect you to know if you can sing and which section you belong. I went right to the alto section because that's what I sang throughout high school. I'm tall, so I naturally moved to the back of the horse-shoe-shaped room. The room was small and packed.

I happened to stand behind identical twin sisters. It was crazy. Not only did they look exactly alike, but they also moved exactly alike, and they sounded exactly alike. I knew their faces from high school, but I didn't know them personally. The gospel choir was one of the few places you could go to see the other Black students on campus. TSC was still a culture shock for me coming from a predominately Black school. I knew the song we were singing, but my notes didn't match anything like the twins. *What? I've sung this song in church, at school, what's up with this?* I tried not to panic as I realized that I matched the girl on my left, so I hung with her hitting my notes. It wasn't until the end of the rehearsal that I learned there was such a thing as first and second sopranos and altos. My instincts served me right in my decision to sing with the lady next to me on the left.

I was still a bit concerned if the director decided to do a typical spot check in each section. I may have stood out because I wasn't always matching the girl next to me. I started having challenges hitting the alto notes and my facial expression was a dead giveaway. I decided to speak up and tell the director that I had sung alto for years in high school, but that I didn't feel like I was cleanly hitting alto notes anymore. During the next rehearsal, I was moved from alto to soprano. Again, since I was awkwardly tall, I took my place on the back row. Once again, I couldn't hit the super high notes like the girl on my right. I must say I felt a lot more comfortable in the soprano section than the alto section, but my voice and those high notes were not seeing eye to eye.

The next rehearsal I assumed the same spot and couldn't hit all the notes again. I took it upon myself and moved back to the alto section. The director immediately stopped and said, "Joi, what are you doing?"

"Well, I didn't belong over there. I don't belong over here. So I'm just trying to figure out where I fit in." There was no shame in my game. I could not hit those high notes and I wasn't afraid to admit it. I didn't want to be singing next to someone who constantly put their finger in their ear to ensure they were on key. That gesture let me know that I was throwing them off key. The director started laughing. She asked me where I was just standing. I named the two girls I was standing in-between. She then replied, "Joi they are first sopranos. Step to the left a little and you should match up with that section. They are the second sopranos."

"So I won't have to hit those notes that are up in the rafters?" I asked.

"No Joi, but if you are comfortable with the beginning of the build in the song then that represents where the second sopranos end the song, so you should not have any trouble." *Me a soprano?* My dad always told me that I was an alto.

I guess my high school music teacher was right, I should have tried the soprano section. I was now excited to finish out this rehearsal because I had finally found my home within the gospel choir. We had some powerhouse voices in our choir and some crowd favorites over the years, and with every choir, there is always an issue of who gets a solo. I always wanted to try out for one, but when you are a little shy and have never sung solo to a large crowd, I figured, *why bother?* Solo selections really became an issue during my junior year. I was still afraid to speak up and was relieved that others were bickering about it, which meant that I was not even in the running.

By my senior year, it was such a big deal that the director decided to give a first crack at solos to folks who had *never* sung that were seniors. *Really! Really? I'm not pressed for a solo. I don't have nothing to worry about. They can fight all they want.* The director announced that she had written her first song, "I Am," and that she needed a soprano vocalist to sing lead. As a senior in the second soprano section, she wanted *me* to sing it. I can't say I remember how this all went down, but I can say that there was an apple in my throat and I was sick to my stomach. I loved to sing in the choir, but this was a cruel joke. *Who does this? Are Y'all trying to embarrass me? What's up with this? Really? I just so happen to be the senior up for this? The other young lady they were considering was having extensive issues with her vocal chords, but somehow this landed on my plate. Really? The director's first song? No pressure Joi.*

Stephanie, the director went on to give background on why she wrote the song, the Scripture reference, and the melody. Stephanie was a *real* singer. She could hit every riff under the sun and ad lib like the best of them. What was she expecting me to do with this song? I felt sick to my stomach for days, but I practiced and practiced. In the back of my mind I kept feeling like this was a set up. It just so happened that this semester the popularity of the choir was continuing to expand and we were being asked to sing at different events on campus.

You guessed it. Stephanie wanted her song sung at *all* of these events. I was not a confident songstress that blew you out of the water. I sang with more of a light, airy voice. If people were really moved during the song, the director and I would go back and forth as she threw in some ad libs to the song. We sang "I Am" so much that I used to purposely delay my arrival after class to events hoping that they sang the song before I got there. I convinced myself, *she could lead her own song with no problem.* Sure enough, she always waited for me to arrive. There was no getting out of it. The song was soon added to the list for our big gospel event where we invited several choirs on campus to worship together.

Why on Earth is she doing this to me? I thought. *Stephanie are you kidding me? Really? Haven't we sung this enough?* The answer was no. This was her song and we were singing it and I was leading it, no questions asked. I sang at the gospel event to the surprise of my parents and my stepfather. Singing a solo at this event was a big deal. My stepfather was so impressed that the next day he called to congratulate me on a job well done. He suggested that I take music lessons to learn how to deal with my nerves. He said that it would help me polish up the voice that he knew was inside of me. *Lord, what in the world is going on with all this? First you have me singing this song all over campus. Then I get to the final performance of a major gospel event which was an amazing experience like none that I had ever had before. Now my stepfather is encouraging me to pursue singing to the extent that he is offering to pay for it! Lord, please lead me and guide me. My stepfather told me don't delay in calling a music school down here and get it done. Do I want to sing? Yes. Do I believe I can sing? Yes. Do I know where else I might sing after college? No. Now that I sang at our final event will I sing again? I'm just gonna pray on this and see how I feel in a few days.*

Since I had an extra semester before graduation, I took my step-father up on vocal lessons since he was paying for it. I went in for the vocal assessment. I shared with the woman that I thought I was an alto and was moved this past year to the soprano section of the choir. After working with the vocal coach she identified that I was a mezzo-soprano. I had to look that one up. "Mezzo," Okay, that meant second-soprano.

I never told my dad what the woman said about my voice. He asked me what songs I was singing for my recital and I told him. He looked at me kind of strange. He knew they were soprano songs, but when I came home and sang around him, I still sang the alto parts. He was just gonna have to see for himself at the recital. I wanted him to eat his words and finally see that I *am* a soprano. My dad sang in communitunity choirs and church choirs for years. He is a second bass: the one with that really deep voice. He started doing musical theater with me after I graduated from college. We had a great time doing a Rock N Roll Review Reunion show years ago. We actually did a rehash of the show 10 years later for the community and both sides of my family attended.

I was taking lessons at the Trenton Conservatory of Music. The building looked like the haunted house from the old TV show, "The Munsters." I remember walking upstairs and the stairs creaked. I felt proud to be taking music lessons, singing above a whisper, and being open to critique. This was a new feeling and real growth for me. For years, I wasn't singing in the right vocal section. I learned how easy it was to stay on key when you are singing in the right voice part. This music class was opening my mind to an interesting concept; *Joi can actually sing and she is a soprano!*

I recall the one time I did tell my father about one of my lessons and the teacher told me that I was a soprano and he'd insist that I wasn't. When I told him what song I was working on in my lessons he'd tell me he thought that might be too high for me. Then for whatever reason my boyfriend at the time, sided with my dad. He doesn't even know vocal tone or being on or off key. Now, he was telling me what I couldn't do and what I couldn't sing. Using phrases like, "Well your father said … And he knows music." Although I loved to sing, I stopped singing around both of them. There were times when I would slip up and start singing in the car and my dad would say, "See you're not a soprano, you would need to sing that higher if you were a soprano." I was tired of the two of them telling me what they thought I was or was not.

I later shared the names of the songs for my recital and my father questioned the music teacher's song choice. My dad never really heard me sing except in a car and around the house. The best way to deal with my father was to show him. After the recital, he handed me a rose and said it was a perfect song choice, and shared that he didn't know I could hit those high notes. My boyfriend was not there for the recital, but when my father's language began to change about my being a soprano so did his. All of these musical experiences got me to the place where I would confidently say to my birth mom or anyone else that I can sing! This was huge for me. I never shared that with folk. As it was rolling off my lips, I knew that if I said it, I'd have to own it now and forevermore.

February 12, 2018

Hearing my birth mother Flo's voice at the opening of church service for the first time was one thing. Hearing her sing was another. I could not listen to her and watch her sing at the same time. It was an emotional overload. After she sung the first few lyrics, my mother leaned in and said, "Now you see where you get your voice from." I was totally blown away. My father heard her and he agreed. Wow! Flo sang, "Worth," by Anthony Brown and Group Therapy. Lyrically, the song was enough to make me run out the church crying my eyes out, but I had to sit still and take in this surreal moment.

> *"You thought I was worth saving*
> *So, You came and changed my life*
> *You thought I was worth keeping*
> *So, You cleaned me up inside*
> *You thought I was to die for*
> *So, You sacrificed your life*

So, I could be free
So, I could be whole
So, I could tell everyone I know

The final stanza of this song as I listened now and reflected on her experience as a birth mother had a whole new meaning.

Because I am free
Because I am whole
And I will tell everyone I know..

You thought I was to die for
You sacrificed your life
So, I can be free..."
Worth, Anthony Brown

Needless to say, I was an emotional wreck. Flo was singing alto, contralto and hit a few bass notes. She had great control and a much lower register than me. We sing "Worth" in my church choir and it is on my playlist. After I heard Flo sing it, I now listened to it lyrically from a different perspective. I wonder if she and I will sound as good as me and my daughters. I'm actually looking forward to doing a duet with her one day. We've got some singing folks in our family. I think a huge plus for me on my father's side of the family is their appreciation of the arts. I am finally comfortable allowing my singing gift to make room for me.

THE JOY OF MOTHERHOOD, MARRIAGE & DIVORCE

10

It's Official!

I met my husband Gary in college. He and I loved sports, music, and movies. *Flatline* was our first date. It wasn't until the movie started that I realized it was a scary movie. Before I went, everyone told me that it wasn't going to be that scary. In the opening, I realized what flat line referred to—that line which goes across the electrocardiogram machine before you are pronounced dead. After that movie, Gary tried to calm my nerves, but I was too scared to go to sleep. I was pissed. I don't do scary movies and I surely don't do them before bedtime. We decided to watch *Coming to America* for laughs.

When I visited his dorm room, the only items he brought from home in South Carolina was a black bag, a yellow comforter, and a pillow. He did not have anything. I was working when we began dating. I started buying him things that he needed: shoes, sneakers, clothes, toothpaste, grooming and hygiene supplies. I worked and always had a paid internship. At the time, I was working for DYFS in Trenton as a youth advocate. My job was to help teens get on the right path in life and teach them social skills. We were both interested in the law and the kids in this program came to the program through a court order, so there was a loose connection. Gary did well with kids and when we went back to my home in Plainfield we took out my little cousins, so he seemed like a good candidate. I eventually got him a job at DYFS. Sometimes he had to take kids out and I accompanied him. We took the kids to the movies, playground, dinner, bowling, or wherever we decided was a great experience. It was all about teaching life skills in a real-world environment.

We were both criminal justice majors and he always talked about his desire to do well in life so that one day he could help his nieces and nephews back home. It was that character trait that connected us early in our relationship. He wanted to do so much more for his nieces and nephews and I loved doing things with my little cousins. Working with these kids in the youth advocate program gave us the opportunity to see each other in a different light. Most of the kids had family members caught up in the prison system or they were at risk of being in the system themselves.

It was through my work experience that I learned about poverty, mental health issues, work ethic, social work, budgeting, and the importance of paying bills on time. Walking into a home one evening with eight kids living in one home was mind-blowing. I had never seen candles, extension cords, and cables coming through the window from the house next door. I was a college student who spent too much money on clothes I didn't need. These kids' situation made me look at life very differently. It made me realize the importance of an education. Five of the eight kids sat around a TV who were meeting me for the first time. They were just talking to me like this was normal. I soon learned that this was actually *their* normal. It was one of the family's monthly routines as bills were not always paid on time, so the electricity was one of the necessities to get cut off. One of them responded, "Oh payday is coming soon." I had to remind myself from that point forward, *FYF- Fix Your Face Joi. You can't come up in these kids homes with a look of shock, fear, or judgment. You can't be upset because you were only assigned to one of the eight kids. You were hired to do what the courts are requiring you to do. Help make the most of it for this one.* I just hoped and prayed that this wouldn't create a divided household because when I left the home with one child, each time I'd hear the younger kids asking the older sibling why they couldn't come with us. It was this experience that made me realize that I may love working with kids more than I'd allowed myself to believe. *Should I be considering education as my major instead of criminal justice?*

As our relationship developed, my parents seemed to like Gary.

He could talk to my father about sports from any era and he knew what he was talking about. He could talk about health issues with my mom because he said his family *owned* a pharmacy and my mom was a nurse. When he started telling stories about some of the things that his family did in South Carolina, my mother became leery. She suspected he was lying. Especially when my mother went with us down south to visit his family. He said his family owned a pharmacy, but his mother actually *worked* in a pharmacy. After I saw where and how they lived, I assumed his lies were told more out of embarrassment. He didn't expect that we would ever travel south to visit his family. My mom confirmed with his mom that the story about the pharmacy wasn't true. *Why didn't I end the relationship after that trip?*

I thought his desire to develop himself, improve his life, and work to help his family were honorable, so I stuck with my rationale, *He's just embarrassed and he was creating a story that wouldn't bring attention to his family's struggles. When he realizes that what he has or doesn't have isn't important to me as long as I know he is hustling to make a difference, I believed he would stop making up these types of stories.*

We enjoyed talking about our dreams for the future. I thought some of Gary's dreams were far-fetched, but who am I to limit a person's dreams for their future? We were always talking about ways to better ourselves to improve the likelihood of a more prosperous future. It was because of all the wonderful discussions around topics like these that drew me to him. I really thought he'd be a great addition to our family.

Not only could he talk with my dad, but my four uncles loved sports, so Gary would have no problem fitting in with them either. As a lover of sports Gary read and retained information like no one I'd ever seen. His memory was amazing. He would often mention remembering being in his mother's womb which was a hilarious story he told when he had a captive audience. Then years later when he began to challenge my memory during some of our final arguments, I realized that Gary *actually* believed he remembered his womb experience, and those weren't jokes after all. Each argument that occurred near the end of our marriage brought to mind comments he made during the early years that just seemed funny. Now it's 16 plus years later I realize that those wacky assertions were his true thoughts.

We were nearing my last semester when Gary and I agreed that we needed to figure out if we were going to maintain our relationship. I was finishing up my last semester and he told me that he needed to complete another year of school. Before I moved back home, we got engaged. Then a few months after the engagement I was pregnant. I always refer to Jasmin as the engagement baby. I guess we celebrated too much with our decision to get married. Although I finished school in December, I graduated the following June. Gary stayed with me at my mom's often. Then we were living together. Now I knew that he had another year of school, but I was glad to have him around. He was a hustler and always looking for work, and often worked two or three jobs. Yet I knew in our field that having the degree was most import-ant so I was pushing for him to finish college.

Months later his transcript arrived. I was trying to figure out if he had a year or more than a year to complete. I was excited when I saw the transcript. I called him at work and told him it arrived. I asked him if I could open it. Privacy was big for me, so I wanted him to know before I ripped it open. I never wanted him opening my mail. When I called, he was in the middle of something at work and insist-ed that I did not open it. It was not until a year after our separation that my mother came across the envelope and we discovered that he failed out of school. All that time we were planning our wedding and talking about our future while he was hanging out on campus— he was technically not a student. WOW! That was mind-blowing. That's when I was immediately taken aback to the arguments over his tran-script. This explains why he never wanted me to apply for his college transcript. This is why he would never remember to get the money order for the transcript.

In the midst of wedding planning which was around the time his transcript arrived, you would think he would bring that up as soon as he came home and saw the transcript. Nope. He always had a way of talking his way around not going back to school. Years later, after the separation when he was calling and leaving me nasty messages and continuing to call me a liar, my first thought was, *why bother bringing it up? It was no use anyway.* My second thought was *since he's constantly telling me I'm a liar, let me drop this transcript jewel on him so that he knows that I know he is a fake!* My third thought was, *what difference would it make at this stage of the game? Why in the world did he fail all those courses?* Gary could tell me things about the classes and the reading assignments like clockwork. He knew the material. I began to pay attention to his writing and old notebook entries from work and soon realized that his poor writing skills may have had something to do with it. But none of that came up until a heated argument, his false accusations, and calling me a liar until I finally had enough. His words hit me to the core. *How dare you?* Game on. So in the midst of that argument, it all came out. He quickly changed the subject.

Smooth Operator

Gary was definitely a charmer and could talk to anybody about anything. Since he was so outgoing, I did not have to be. I jumped into conversations sporadically. I loved the excitement of listening and watching his conversations with unusual people. Over the years, I started losing my voice because he dominated the conversation and it became his opinion or nothing. While I initially thought our pairing complimented us, I realized that I was furthering the distance in starting conversations with people. I was so out of practice that I'd get social anxiety just knowing an event was coming up. The work-related events I could handle with no problem, but in personal social settings, I'd clam up and there was dead silence.

On top of that, I had to overcome this "thing" in the black community that light-skinned girls are stuck up and don't speak to people. So I had to deal with this double-edged sword. I was shy in social settings, but outgoing in work-related events which created an imbalance of who I really am. I wondered, *where had little Joi gone?* The girl whose mother could hear her down the block from the school talking on the playground during recess. I was loud and always talking. My mom could tell me what I said word-for-word. *Where is the girl who was fierce enough to play flag football with the boys every morning?* I really wanted her back, but I didn't have the courage to speak up and fight for her voice.

Realizing my shortcomings, it was always important to me that my girls did not lean on others to be the initiators of conversation. In every way possible, I knew that I could not allow Jasmin to grow up thinking that my fear of conversation and lack of interaction with people is correct behavior. She didn't understand it then, but when she and her sisters got older, I told them how I loved their father's ability to meet strangers and I wanted to nurture that trait in all of them. I didn't want them to develop my social anxiety habits. So whether at church or at school, if the girls saw a lady and said they liked her dress or her hair, I made sure they voiced that compliment to the person at that moment. I always told them, "Sometimes a compliment can make a person's day. So why don't we try to be the first?"

There was nothing in Gary's name. I was the breadwinner in our house. Yet he had his family thinking that he was making celebrity-type money with sports and clients, but the girls and I were spending *all* of his money, so there was not much left to send to them in South Carolina. He always bragged that he could call on this person or that person, but the one cousin who was a business owner rarely called him. When we visited his family for the holidays and the girls had music or video players, Gary would tell the other kids in his family that he would buy them the same things for the next holiday. Jasmin and Traci did not want to say anything to embarrass him, because they knew that he wasn't working and it was mommy who was *really* buying them the things they needed and the toys as well.

On other occasions, I never knew exactly what he told his family about our living situation. Every now and then I'd hear an empty promise or a partial truth mixed with a lie. He had that down to a science. There were always some parts of what he was saying that were absolutely true, especially with the sports agency opportunity, but then the other parts about landing deals or signing contracts were absolutely false. His family believed most of the stories because they were aware of Marlon, the *one* player from their hometown who made his way on to the practice squad of the Washington Redskins. However, what no one knew was that Gary never got any money from Marlon's contract. Gary told me that since the players didn't make a lot on the practice squad, he felt Marlon should keep the commission he would have earned.

One evening over dinner during Marlon's visit to our home, Gary wanted both me and Marlon to hear him talking to individuals from Bad Boy Records' office. It was during the time Puffy was interested in starting a sports agency. Gary had been communicating with Puffy's office and writing proposals to land a deal. That's when he put his dream team together of people with brains and power. His team had a great proposal. Puffy's office was calling every night, well after midnight. Records and giveaways were being delivered to the house on a regular basis. I know for a fact that Gary was really in connection with his office. Yet I always wondered why in the world they sent records. Did they think he had a radio station? I heard several of the conversations and I saw the packages. *Gary knew sports, he studied athletes, he studied teams needs, all he needed was an opportunity*, I thought. When he talked sports his face lit up. So many parts of his efforts and stories were true, but any mention of lucrative financial incomes was definitely false.

He was constantly interacting with general practitioner lawyers, financial advisors, entertainment lawyers, and several business owners.

Gary pitched ideas to them, and many were on board to help gain Puffy's interest to have a Bad Boy startup team its new sports management branch. He has a very creative mind and often pitched the same ideas to different people to see who would bite first. He tried the same thing with Queen Latifah's people, but he never got as far with her team as he did with Puffy. All of the people on Gary's dream team were already successful in their field. He had convinced them that sports management was a booming opportunity. Again. I saw evidence of work being done, evidence of meetings, agendas, and proposals. Presentations were being created collaboratively, but nothing ever panned out.

For months, Gary went to celebrity events in New York and stayed out late. I was happy to confirm his stories of grandeur to my parents and others because I was speaking the truth based on my knowledge, but again, not one dollar manifested. Some days it felt good that Gary was finding a path to a new career. Then it got to the point when I realized that he was *pretending* to go work. I only found out because he was still home when my father rode by our block. My dad always passed through and checked the house since at the time we lived in my dad's house. He saw Gary home on too many occasions and finally confronted him, only to find out that he was not working.

Then job options became few and far between and he was always *looking* for a job. When he did have a job, we never heard when he got fired or if he just walked out. He said he would get a second job to bring in money, but did not think that he could work at a store, or work late nights or during holiday hours for stockers. While he felt that he could have two jobs, he always believed his skills were far too advanced for Walmart or a fast food joint. He was still hanging on to the sports management thing, even though people were slowly starting to pull away from him for reasons that I couldn't figure out. He stopped calling people who were his friends and they did not call him. Then out of nowhere, he stopped talking about Puffy. The records and giveaways came to an end. That's when I knew something was up, but there was no way for me to find out.

After nothing materialized with the sports management and a host of other businesses, I saw his pattern. He used his charm to talk to people about my profession in education and beamed about all of the activities that the girls were involved with. In hindsight, it painted a picture of stability, working in honest professional fields, and being a doting father. The average guys he'd play basketball with on Saturday and Sunday for years didn't know he was my husband, but yet those working for high profile celebrities knew about me and our daughters. I started to feel that it was his half-truth and half-lies that people eventually started to see through. Gary had some really good ideas and was at the table with high profile people, but I always thought I missed something in this equation or maybe his fakeness shined brighter to outsiders.

Although, in hindsight, Gary's employment efforts look like a calculated game. It felt like he was really working and trying to get the sports management business going. It was something he could be good at because he knew sports like the back of his hand. I wanted to support him. I could hear him talking to parents, coaches, and to businesses for endorsements. Now I know why he always made sure that I heard him by talking on speaker phone often. That was his bragging point, *Oh, I was talking to Reebok or Footlocker, Joi you heard them. Puffy's office calling every night.* I was able to cosign on all the things I heard him say to people.

In the early 2000s, Gary had a few different jobs. He did well at an office supply company selling office supplies. For exceeding his sales goals he won a trip for the two of us to Cancun. Then he told management that he wanted to be more competitive, so he targeted New York hospitals to take their business accounts from competitors. He outbid the competitors and was constantly battling with management over discounts. As with every company that he left or was fired, he blamed everyone for his woes. He said that others at the company were stealing his connections and taking his work. He wanted to offer 70% off all items. He did not understand the issues his bosses were having with this discount. He was furious. Based on his calculations, they could still make a lot of money if he had *all* of the New York health and hospitals on this same account. So he left.

He went to another company and convinced them that he had connections and could bring in great business. The new bosses said his percentages were off. This happened in three different companies! After finding yet another new company I asked him if he did the calculations because there was no way three different companies under three different management heads could have their numbers wrong. I told him that there had to be something wrong with his calculations and his steep 70% discount.

I had trained on Microsoft Excel and was very good at it. Gary gave me 20 -30 pages on an Excel spreadsheet and asked me to calculate the percentages. I copied his file, changed the percentages to calculate the profit, and every item in the profit column turned negative. Every bid would make the company lose money and the hospital had already accepted his bid. He got upset and said that I was siding with the company and really didn't know what I was talking about and that he would never ask me anything again! He refused to agree that his numbers would make every company bankrupt. After those interactions, I realized why he couldn't keep a job. He was literally going from company to company with bids that would have put them out of business.

Again, always a hustler, and in-between bids for hospitals and selling various products, he sold office furniture to police stations and state agencies in the City of Newark. He was also rehabbing homes and submitting bids for row houses. He was setting up office furniture in the local police headquarters. He had accounts with the historic homes in Newark and helped remodel the furniture. Again we knew this was true because he took us on after-hours tours of places and spent hours studying catalogs with various products. *But where was the money?*

I admit that I did not have a great understanding of sales, but his commissions just didn't add up. Then he started saying that the company messed up on his commission check and they would fix it the next time around. After the separation, I can only guess that he used the money on drugs. I also learned that he was sending child support payments to the child's mother that he *swore* the blood test revealed was not his child. His checks were inconsistent. He always had a story for how he was using his money.

11

Drugs, Lies, and Divorce

I knew Gary smoked weed every now and then. I found a flour sack sized bag in his desk one night. When I was ready to bring it up and ask him about it, the bag was gone the next day. He never came home smelling like marijuana—no, never had that stink skunk smell on him. My discovery happened a few months after our separation. The girls and I were cleaning the garage. I came upon a large white plaster bucket that showed me that all of those nights of working out in the garage were not weight-lifting sessions at all. As I went to the shelf to move the bucket, I expected it to be heavy. I lifted it easily. I wanted to open it to see if it was something that needed to be salvaged or if I could just toss it. I pulled the lid off and there were aluminum foil sheets— hundreds of them to be exact, in this white bucket.

Then there were pieces of paper burnt in the center of the folded foil sheets. As I opened the foil on a few of them I saw ashes. Then I got to a few where the papers hadn't fully burned. One piece of paper had names and dates of the people "following" him. Another paper had one of the guys' names who he thought I had an affair with. This was creepy. I folded them back. I wasn't sure what I was looking at and both the girls were in the garage. I could talk to Jasmin about this, but not Tasha, at least not yet. During this time, Tasha was still in la-la land, and I was not sure if she understood the magnitude of our trials and tribulations living in this house under these circumstances. That's because the girl was always sleeping! I'm pretty sure she thinks we make up a lot of this stuff up.

Tasha also doesn't like to clean, so I was sure she wouldn't mind me telling her to go into the house. I told Tasha to take a break. She had no problem with that idea and complained that the garage was hot. I felt kind of stupid at that the moment as I'm old enough to know better, but I really didn't know what I was looking at. I knew this had something to do with drugs and I knew that you don't need aluminum foil to smoke marijuana. So I called Jasmin back into the garage. I showed her the bucket and we tried to figure it out by doing an online search. We Googled: "How can aluminum foil be used for drugs?"

What an eye-opening search! There are people on Youtube who were actually showing you exactly what to do. There is a burn spot on the foil and in the video and it was cocaine. The people in the video smoked and created their own pipe. *Oh Lord, are you telling me that I was living with a crackhead? Is that why he started having teeth issues? Is that why he was having these hallucinations and odd behaviors? How can he afford this? Is this where his money and checks were going all these years? Does crack have a certain smell that I wasn't aware of? This bucket is full - What the HELL?* I tried to figure out who I could confide in and then I decided to ask a friend who is in law enforcement. He took it to a friend who worked in narcotics and it tested positive for cocaine and he said it was crack cocaine. Wow! My garage discovery put a lot of his behaviors into perspective. I was sick to my stomach. *How did I not know he was smoking crack? That explains his never having money and I guess why he didn't smell like weed. That explains why no new muscles were forming with all those nights working out in the garage.* In the video, the participants mentioned that they save the remnants for when they are broke and they can go back and use them later. I cried for hours. I was pissed. I had to be the most naive person in the world. Here I thought keeping him around at least gave the girls a chance to have their father in their lives. *Stupid Joi, just stupid. Did you need him that much in your life or would you have been better off without him? What were you thinking? Every sign, every symptom, based on my research, I could now check off. Crackhead explains it all!*

Before I found out about the drug use, I did not realize the signs: teeth falling out, paranoia, highs and lows and everything that we had been seeing all lined up with him using these drugs. *How could I not have known that this was going on? Was it happening in the house? Garage?* The girls always said he smoked outside a lot. When they came home from school they said he would tell them not to tell me because I'd be mad at him. He told them it was his favorite *cigars* and I don't want Joi to know. The discovery of that crack bucket sent me back to therapy. Now I was feeling guilty for having kept him around. When the girls were in middle school they would always say *"You know you can divorce him, he doesn't help you. He's your fourth child. MOMMY, he DOESN'T HELP you!"*

Reflecting on the impact drugs and the alcohol had on his system, I am fortunate that it never got to physical abuse, but we were always on eggshells because we never knew what triggered the mood swings. Early on, when I thought it was marijuana, I often preferred him high. He was less aggressive and less confrontational. The effects of alcohol varied and his drinking led me to drink less and I hated the smell of beer. It was a scent that immediately triggered anger. Those nights when he came home reeking of beer were often the most verbally abusive and accusatory arguments that ended up in lots of apologies, his crying, and wanting to be affectionate. I absolutely hated the smell and his attempts to be affectionate after the nasty comments were sickening. In those moments, I didn't care if a lack of intimacy leads him astray. I was trying to give him away. So when people say they can't go without intimacy, just let someone try to take something from you when you are not open to it you will learn how to shut off that biological and emotional switch with no problem.

We went years without a touch, without a kiss. *Don't come near me. Don't touch me. Stay on your side of the bed.* Constantly smelling of alcohol made it even easier to keep me at a distance. After the separation, I had to retrain my brain not to equate the smell of alcohol with an argument brewing. That is something I'm still struggling with. I immediately get angry and I'm constantly talking to myself. *Joi, this isn't him. It's okay to drink and enjoy one another. There is no argument. There is no aggressive behavior. RELAX and enjoy the moment. YOU are okay! HE IS NOT HIM.* Triggers... I had to learn over time what my triggers were. I'm learning not to let them control my reactions to things. I'm learning to change my thinking. A lot of the talking throughout this book is actually me talking to myself and talking to God.

Gary was either hot or cold. The nice guy or the mean guy. The girls and I stayed away from home on many days until we knew he was gone. After a while, it became easier because we started to realize how much he never actually came home. Now that he was gone, we stopped hanging out so much at my mothers. She had to know something odd was going on, but she never asked. She could definitely see that he helped with nothing. I was constantly on the go. Had it not been for my mother during those times, I would not have been able to maintain any sense of normalcy with the girls. We talk about it now when we are sitting around the house. It is more evident to us now that the house is packed and full of life. The girls can now have their friends over; it is so clear how unhealthy our home was in the past. Gary always said, "People can't stand us!" He told us that everybody hated us and were out to get us. He created an element or a sense of fear. He'd make a scene, argue, and be rude to anyone who came over. The girls were embarrassed. For them, it became easier just to not have company.

He was suspicious of everyone. It went from sounding like safety concerns with good intentions to being suspicious of everyone because they were all out to get us. There was something wrong with them and something wrong with their parents. So when he did get along with and like any of my friends or colleagues, it made my life much easier. There was nothing to argue about. I thought it was jealousy. If there was no stamp of approval, any interaction with that person caused an argument. My mind would always go back to those early days where he warned me about a few characters to stay away from and he was *always* right. I hated that. I leaned on his intuition of people more than I did my own. After a while, I got tired of hearing, "I told you so Joi. You didn't listen. I see you want to learn the hard way and look at what happened. Isn't that exactly what I told you would happen?" So my thinking became, *if he saw something, it must be something that I'm overlooking.* In the past, we never had people at the house unless I was tired of his antics and felt like arguing with him which made him leave the house anyway.

Please Excuse Him

The weekends were usually filled with activities for the girls. Traci had a few of her teammates over after her basketball game. During all of the games, Gary talked to her teammates' dads and high-fives them at every game without fail. Yet if her friends came over after a game, there was a huge issue. The girls and I had to sit through lectures of who we couldn't trust. In hindsight, I wonder if this impacted the girls in making friends? It had to because the person he appeared to be in public was not the same person behind closed doors in our home.

Our usual response amongst ourselves was, "Where is he getting that information about our friends and their parents from? Why would people say that about us?" These are the people Gary was sitting and laughing with all season. In my mind, *What happened from the last basketball game up to now?* His favorite line to the girls was, "You know they don't like your mother and father. They want what we have. Everybody is jealous of what we have." I always found this hilarious because the truth of the matter is that he had absolutely nothing! If I put him out that day, he would only have the clothes on his back that I bought him. He talked a whole lot of mess to people leading them to believe he was worth something.

One evening, Jasmin brought over a young man she was dating and two of his cousins. Traci had recently broken up with her boyfriend. They were having a breakup party! Gary walked into the living room and was rude to them from the moment they came in the door. It was always the same negative rhetoric. Gary and I were standing near the front door. The argument ensued, "Joi, what were we thinking about allowing boys to come over? Their families don't even like us and they're talking about us!" The girls could hear him in earshot.

"Look, if you have a nasty attitude, then go upstairs! You don't know them nor their parents!" That silenced him for a moment because he didn't know them. The girls had the best break up party ever. There was lots of laughing and dancing. Our argument continued and he started with typical insults, "How stupid could you be?" I hated those words. Fortunately, I heard the laughter from downstairs throughout the house, *You're not stealing my joy. You don't know these boys. Do us a favor and stay upstairs or leave? How about just leave because I'm done with this conversation. Argue with yourself.*

We continued arguing for a few more minutes. Then I stopped responding. He eventually grabbed his things and left. *Thank Goodness! I hope these girls and those boys didn't hear all that.* I returned to the living room and they are now playing games. I stood in the entrance thinking, *I'll take his argument for this. This is their home. Why shouldn't they have company? How do I get him past these delusions? This is more than jealousy. What the heck is this?*

One day after the separation, I heard one of the girl's friends say, I never knew you had this type of family. We were dancing and singing in the family room. And Jasmin quickly responded, "We couldn't have company before. You weren't allowed come over!" Just as matter of factly as that. Her answer startled him a bit, but Jasmin kept it moving and didn't skip a beat. They were enjoying having company since they had not had friends over in a long time.

Full Circle

When I think about the things that Gary thought he owned or what he claimed over the years, I know now that he has no control over it. I learned so much about the man I married after the relationship was over. There were so many half-truths over the twenty-year time span that I'm still in shock and retracing conversations over the years that were half-truths. I think about the type of person who could maintain the art of lies for so long and I see someone pretty messed up inside.

I think about how we always talked about church. We went to a few churches during the course of our marriage always trying to find the best fit for both of us and the children. He was very supportive when I was singing with the gospel choir. Very encouraging as I began to learn about the voice inside of me. He always made me feel safe. In his presence, I always felt like he was protecting me. That later turned into a negative action when he began to make me feel like if he wasn't around something terrible would happen to me. A large part of what attracted me to him was that he was a Christian and he knew the Bible. He knew Scriptures and verses to refer to when I was down. He was very caring and confident in everything that he did. He was a hustler and always trying to figure out how to help someone out. He would find ways to make ends meet; customer service, cleaning service, youth advocate he was hustling.

As the years went on, I never felt safe in his presence. I wondered what he might do to me in my sleep. Prayer, especially after a verbal altercation or after one of his many accusations was the only thing that got me through to the next day and the day after. *Who could I tell that I was afraid of my husband?* If I told someone then I'd have to explain all of the million reasons why. I'd have to explain all of the negative and horrible things he said to me, and about me to our closest friends. Most friends didn't know that I knew he spewed his stupid accusations about me to them. Or I don't think they knew. Even now, I find out that people would often talk to one another trying to figure out why he would do such a thing. *Who tells people that their wife has a disease? Who tells people that their wife is messing around with other people?* Of course, if it's your boys and you have this inkling about your woman cheating, but to say random things to targeted people was just mind-blowing.

For the most part, I realized that I was just trying to wait until his other personality showed up so that we could get past this moment. Where was that happy guy that made me laugh? That guy who would dance and sing off key just to make me smile after a bad day at work. I had a hard time rationalizing what my mind and body were going through at that time; moody, jumpy, and nervous.

I think about our college days when every time we broke up or we both went out with other people, he always told me why that person was not right for me, and each time he was right. Then we were back together again. I had so many situations with other people and he was always the one I came back to.

While I love music, there was a Stevie Wonder song, "Make Sure You Are Sure?" that Gary played when we dated to win me over to make me question breaking up with him. I hate this song to this day. He would even sing the version of it from the *Harlem Nights* movie. By end of his song and our conversation, he convinced me that I wasn't sure if I wanted to break up with him. He played it on cassette until the tape popped. If I hear it today, I'm walking out. A song should not have that much power over you, but we had plenty of arguments with that song in the background—real facts! *God thank you for ending my relationship with Gary. Thank you for the gift of my three wonderful daughters. I am absolutely "sure!" I finally had the courage to file for divorce and that was the best thing for my future and anyone connected to me. Lord, I thank you. I've got my joy back!*

After my divorce lawyer heard one of the voice messages Gary left on her business phone, and heard about the conversations her secretary had with him, she started putting together pieces of our marriage. I shared emails Gary sent to our pastor and to me during our separation. Her secretary was afraid that he would show up at the office. Kisha tried to keep her composure as she sat in her chair. She heard at least five to seven more of the messages he was leaving on my voicemail at work. I sat there speechless. Those messages were difficult to hear and they haunt me to this day. The rants of truth and lies all mixed together from someone I once loved made me sick to my stomach. She paused and took a deep breath. She looked at me with her head tilted to the side. She had that look like she didn't believe what she had just heard. I knew it was a lot to soak in. I tune out anytime I had to play those messages for someone.

After a long pause, she said, "My hat is off to you. To just look at you, I would never think this is what you are going through." Then she said, "I know you are not ready now, but when you are, I look forward to reading your book."

"It's funny you say that, he wanted me to put in our divorce agreement that I would not write a book about him." After an argument when he saw me writing that evening or the next day he'd go ballistic and started yelling, "Joi, don't write no f___ song, don't write no f____ book. Don't write sh__ about me. YOU HEAR ME. I mean it!"

When he was pissed my blood boiled because his tone was harsh. It made me cringe. He often spits as the words poured out of his lips." *Who would ever think about writing a book about this? I'd be too embarrassed to tell people I allowed you to put me through this.* Then these thoughts were running through my head, *I allowed you to live here for years without contributing, I accepted your B.S. about working on commission and there was always an issue with payment at the job. I believed someone might be ripping you off. I gave you money like you were my child and yet you allowed your family to think you were this great provider.* Every time he went there about me writing a book, I couldn't even imagine how he came to that thinking. I write for my own personal reasons. The crazy part of it all is that even after arguments with him, I never wrote about it then. All of the times when I was writing about him, he was not around. After years of accusing me of writing about him, I began to think maybe his crazy a$$ is on to something. With every rant, I was so close to saying, "BUT you give me so much f*&&%$# material why wouldn't I consider it!"

I never shouted those words to him because I knew that my response would prolong the argument. So I held my tongue and that made me even more furious. I had learned over the years that when he was a bit off, it was a waste of time to argue because no matter what I said he would somehow flip it to somehow this was my fault. Then he'd go off on the deep end and make his way back to the accusations of me having a disease, seeing other people, the officer, the ball player, or the guy at church. Then it typically ended with apologies for everything he said. Over the years, I learned to just let him wear himself out making up all of his stories, let him argue with himself, ignore him, tune him out, and write about his craziness later. *Don't internalize his mess, Joi. Something is wrong with him.* I just didn't know what it was.

After the separation and years of counseling, I finally accepted the diagnosis of post-traumatic stress disorder (PTSD). It's really not just for people in the military. My therapist explained it to me and I also did my research. Although I had questions, there was no doubt that I was experiencing PTSD. It is a mental health condition triggered by a person experiencing or witnessing a terrifying event. I finally realized that I wasn't crazy and all of the flashbacks, nightmares, anxiety, loud noises, screams, facial expressions, and even body language brought on uncontrollable thoughts and emotions about Gary. There wasn't one PTSD symptom that I didn't have! I could think of fifty-thousand situations that yielded *all* the results on the pages and pages of material that I read.

Relationship expert Harville Hendrix, created the "Goodbye Process" to say to your ex-partner. He emphasized how people move on to other relationships and never really said "goodbye" to the old relationship. In taking his advice, I was relieved to shout my goodbye for all to hear:

Gary, I'm saying goodbye to criticism, lies, and accusation about extramarital affairs. Lies about your other child or don't have your driver's license. Goodbye to the nightly fears that you will get pulled over leaving me to figure out how to bail you out. Goodbye to being on pins and needles because of your mood swings.

Goodbye to the good stuff: Laughing, dancing, your outgoing personality and your ability to engage complete strangers.

Goodbye to the dream of the marriage: Growing old together, being grandparents together, being the seniors holding hands walking the development together.

Goodbye Gary, for good!

12

My Girls Say the Darndest Things

When the girls were growing up, I could not resist journaling the funny things they said. I actually filled two journals reliving our conversations. Every day, no matter how crazy or stressed I was, one of them found a way to make me laugh. Looking back, I am so thankful to God for all of these moments and memories with each of my girls. They have kept me sane, responsible, and accountable when my life was in chaos.

Jasmin was jumping up and down on the bed saying she had breast. Traci looked at her and replied, "Nope, you have one bean." Tasha joined in, "It's just one Jasmin. Just one!" and they all chuckled.

The next day, Tasha came home from school and said, "Mom, I had to ask my teacher to go to the bathroom because my bra was itching and I needed to scratch." Later on, Tasha said, "My bra is killing me." I asked Tasha to come into the room.

"Show me this bra that you are having an issue with."

She lifted her shirt and yelled, "See!"

I said, "Tasha, you're six. This is actually one of those small t-shirts from when you were about three! It hurts because it is *not* a bra and it is squeezing you. It's the elastic that's making you itch."

She looked at me innocently and said, "Oh, I thought this was a bra."

"What makes you think you need a bra anyway?" I laughed and shook my head.

I was on the phone with my mom and Tasha heard me telling mom the story of when Traci inquired about a butthole. I told mom, that Traci could not remember what her teacher called it. Tasha chimed in, "Oh, Briana calls it a crack!" I have no clue what that lesson in school was about today.

Jasmin was a little upset when she came home. She said, "My math teacher gave me a C/D instead of a B/C." Traci yelled out, "BC, that's Before Christ! How could she give you something then?" I laughed so hard. It was the interim report card time.

I took the girls to open bank accounts. When we left, Jasmin asked which section of the booklet she should start reading first. I said, "The woman mentioned reading the funds available section."

"Mom, I can't find it."

"Look for withdrawals."

Traci jumped in, "Now, why would they be talking about under-wear at the bank?"

"Not *drawls* as we say it. I'm saying WITHDRAWALS."

When Tasha was around four years old, she kept coming back and forth in my room sneaking gum and candy behind my back as I watched TV. Even though I busted her a couple of times she kept coming back. Finally, she asked, "How can you see me? Aren't you watching TV?"

"I sure am." She looked confused. "Didn't you know that teachers have eyes in the back of their heads? All Mom's and teachers have them."

With a strange look on her face, she hesitantly walked up to me.

"Can I see them?"

"No. They only come out when they need to. And they'll catch you every time today."

"Yeah, but where are they?"

"Tasha, you won't be able to see them."

She ran into the room to tell Jasmin and Traci. They laughed. Traci was eight years old and came running into the room. She grabbed my head.

"Let me see!" As she looked at the back of my head and moved my hair, "There's no eyes back there mommy!"

"Traci I will tell you and Tasha, that you won't be able to see them." Traci started brushing through my hair to prove to Tasha that I wasn't telling the truth.

"Look Tasha look. No eyes." Tasha still wasn't convinced.

Standing behind me, Traci said "OK Miss four eyes, how many fingers do I have up?"

"One!" Traci was shocked that I was right.

"Well, we have to try this again. How many now?" Tasha was trying to see her fingers to give me the answer and Tasha said, "three."

I could feel Traci behind me rushing to change the number of fingers she had up. So I said "four." She chimed in and said, "Wrong!"

I cut her off and said, "But I really believe it may have been two."

"Oh yes it's two, but you said four first!"

"Well, you kept changing your fingers on me."

Jasmin walked into the room because she heard us laughing very loud.

"What's going on?"

Traci's head tilted to the side, "Mommy told Tasha she has four eyes!" By now, Tasha's jumping up and down, "She does. She really really does. She has two in the back of her head but we can't see them. Only moms and teachers have them."

Jas had the 'you must be kidding me look' on her face. She then said, "Oh, I've heard that before."

Traci still wasn't convinced. Jas knew better and went along with it and Tasha still wasn't really sure.

Later in the day, we took a ride over a few blocks down the street to my father's house. We were all sitting in the kitchen talking and my dad had company. The girls were eating toast. Tasha finished her toast and was trying to take her sisters toast when my father's friend said, "Don't do that Ta."

Tasha was sitting in her lap, but the woman was looking at us talking with the back of her head facing Tasha. Tasha quickly said, "But how did you see me?"

The woman said, "I've got eyes in the back of my head."

Tasha screamed, "Oh No. Oh No!" She jumped out her lap and started looking at the woman as if she was an alien. All I could do was smile. Her statement and the timing was perfect.

When the girls were in middle school I hated cooking dinner after a long day teaching. Jasmin enjoyed cooking and was taking home economics classes. One night she cooked baked chicken, broccoli, and biscuits. I tried eating her frozen broccoli without saying a word. Traci burst out laughing, "This broccoli is frozen!" Their dad yelled, "EAT IT!" Tasha refused to eat hers. I kept trying to eat a few pieces, not to hurt her feelings.

Then when Jasmin took my plate she noticed that I still had broccoli left. She followed me upstairs and said, "Mommy, if something is ever wrong with my food please tell me." I said, "OK, Jas, the broccoli was cold. How did you cook it?"

"I dumped it in the pot, sprinkled a little salt, and warmed it up."

"So you didn't start with a little water in the pot? Traci was right. You fed us frozen broccoli. Did you read the box at all?"

Traci had her life lesson with the nurse today. In her health class, she saw a time-lapse video which showed the of a girls body. She explained how the video showed female private parts. "Mom, it's a real jungle down there!" Then she showed me a diagram of the vagina and asked, "Do you know how eggs are fertilized?"

I replied, "Do you?"

"Yes, but I didn't think you knew. It's really nasty. Now I know why you don't like eggs!"

Traci came home from her AIDS class and said her favorite words, "I HAVE A QUESTION..." Then she told me, "I asked my school nurse, but she told me to ask my parents and if my parents are uncomfortable then she can tell me." I thought of my mom and I knew that I was going to need a book.

"If you can't get AIDS from kissing, but in sex, you're kissing. So why can you get AIDS from sex and not kissing when you are doing both?"

I pulled out every book I had and the closest one that mentioned sex and showed pictures of when men and women get together. I gave it to her to read. Then she wanted to know if there were nipple-less people in the world.

"Call your grandma, she's a nurse!"

I always agreed to give the girls $0.25 if they get a special part in a play or song, and if they did well, I gave a little extra. Tasha told me to get me $0.50 ready! She had a poem and a song. Before her solo, her dad stopped in the room and said, "Are you ready?" She replied, "I was born ready!"

When we got home, we listened to the tape of her solo. She asked, "Do you hear all the applause for me?"

There were three other soloists *and* a choir. My father said, "Tasha, that's for everyone."

"No, I was the best. The crowd went nuts!" She told my mom that her heart was *beeping* (not beating) like crazy when she looked at all those people, but she put her hands behind her back and sang!

On my mom's fridge, Tasha had given my mom a wide pig and my step-father Maurice, a tall frog, which was her artwork from school. We were over for a visit and Tasha walked up to the fridge and said,

"Oh, you still have these?" and she pointed to the side where my mom proudly displays their artwork.

"Yeah. I still have them."

"I gave you this one (and she pointed to the pig) because it has a body like you." You could hear a pin drop. Tasha continued talking. "And the other one has a body like Maurice."

"Oh, no you didn't just say that Tasha!" my mom said sarcastically.

"Yeah, I did."

Tasha did not realize the depth of her innocent comment. The rest of us fell out on the floor laughing.

"What's so funny?" Tasha asked.

I was telling the girls about my cousin Kelli's birth announcement. Traci said, "So Kelli's pregnant again!" I replied, "Yep."

"So does that mean she has sex?"

"Yes," I answered.

She said, "Nicole too?" (Kelli's sister)

"Yep."

"Oh, that's disgusting! I didn't know they did that!"

Letter from Jasmin

Dear Mama,

Sorry about my journal grade. From now on any grade under 70% I have to get up early to do the dishes, straighten up the downstairs, and walk the dog. One chore will be added every time the extras aren't done.

Can I stay after school on some Thursdays to study with my teachers? Then on every 3rd Thursday of every month, there is a Student Council Meeting. I will make you Proud!

Love,
Your daughter, Jasmin

Tasha ran up on me at Jasmin's poetry night and said, "Mommy, you'd be so proud of Jas. Someone asked her for her cell phone number and she told them she can't give out her number. It's only for emergencies. Aren't you proud? But don't tell her I told you, okay?"

13

Superwoman

"Even when I'm a mess, I still put on a vest with an "S" on my chest..."
- Alicia Keys

I was running myself crazy. Dance classes, piano lessons, voice lessons, karate or taekwondo. I was working late hours as a teacher and running at least three after-school clubs. All of this was going on when I decided to further my degree. I was attending church but not singing regularly and I was beginning to feel like I was losing my identity. I stopped hanging out with my friends and sorority sisters and wasn't fully active in any of my groups and organizations.

Every ounce of what I did was built around my girls and I completely lost myself. I changed positions at my school and really enjoyed my job as I had several years under my belt. My work and life balance were good but none of the activities on the balance side were about me. I was thinking about my career and wondering when I finished my degree what's next? I decided to look through the classifieds one Sunday night. I came across ads for upcoming plays in the area. I was shocked that I had never seen this in the paper before or maybe I just never noticed. I reflected back to a college experience where companies advertised in our college newspaper looking for musicians and singers.

I mustered up the nerve to respond to an ad. I didn't want people to know I was taking voice lessons and trying new things. The audition was for the Mystic Vision Players, at Linden High School for the show, *Anything Goes*. The ad said to come prepared to sing and come prepared to dance and bring tap shoes. I loved tap but thought it would be hilarious since I hadn't tap danced since high school, which was now over twelve years ago. I prayed and said, *Lord if you lead me to this I know you will help me find my tap shoes and get him to stay home with the kids, then I'm meant to go to this audition.*

I've never done musical theater. I have only been singing in church and I prayed that I would find something different to get my creative juices flowing. Somehow today, I land on this ad. *Lord, If you can put the things in place to make it possible to attend this audition then I will accept the challenge.*

As a known pack rat, I tend to group things together. So tap shoes should be with any other items that were used for dance as in my jazz shoes or bodysuits. I looked through stuff in my closet and voilà! There they were. Actually, there was only one shoe. I searched high and low and couldn't find the other one. It was getting late so I stopped searching and prepared my clothes for work. I had a few more days before the audition so I had time to continue my search.

Turns out, when I looked closer at the shoe that I found, I realized it was one of the girls and not mine. That gave me hope that my *two* shoes were together somewhere. I just had to keep looking. My search was successful. I found my tap shoes, my jazz shoes, the girls' old ballet shoes, and my old liturgical dance garments. I hit the jackpot! I tried them on and began tapping around in the bathroom. The old girl still has it. I did a couple of wing steps, a few bells, some flaps and then the girls came running in the bathroom. "What's all that noise?" they asked. "Oh, I pulled out my tap shoes. Mommy is going to audition for a show."

"You still know how to do that? You're not too old for that? How are you going to do that and go to work? Are you trying to be famous?"

These questions and more just rolled out of their mouths. Traci always starts with the questions and then her and Jasmin go back and forth not giving me a moment to answer. When I finally got a word in, I said, "One, no, I'm not too old. Thank you very much. I could out dance either one of you any time, and Two, I'm not trying to be famous. I just need something to do for me. I keep telling you all, I danced from age 4 to age 17, I sang in the choir in high school. I need to do something for me since I keep watching you all do everything I loved to do. So now it's time to see if I can still do them. Plus, I want to try acting to help with my shyness in social settings."

I have always enjoyed the stage, but have never really let go and gone all in. I really feel maybe it's time to sing, dance and act. I told them about the audition and they were very excited. We heard Gary's footsteps and as we were talking. I was trying to end the conversation. Then Traci burst out, "GUESS what Mommy plans on doing?" Before she could get her full thought out, he was putting them out of the bedroom.

Here we go. He started with why there is no time for me to do something like this. He followed up with why I shouldn't expect anyone to help me with the girls running around while I try to do a play because I signed them up for all this mess. So if I could figure out how to do all that by myself and then go to an audition then so be it, because I was told that I was on my own. "Don't ask me to do nothing!" Was his usual line. *Why should I expect anything different?* That night I decided that I wasn't going to argue. I'll do what I normally do; handle my business without him.

Musically
Let's let it all come out
Let's find out what I'm all about
Let's free this thing inside me
Let's let music be my release

I'll share my dreams, I'll share my joys, and I hope these releases will open doors
I've held in so much for all the years of my life
That through writing I'll release all my pain and strife
I now know I have a gift and all the world should see
How God has truly blessed me musically
- ***Joi R. Fisher***

The audition date arrived. I knew Gary would be home but when he saw me packing up my stuff all of a sudden he had somewhere to go. *Okay so now we want to play games, but you know what? I've taken all three of my daughters to a three-hour college class before and they were great, so I am going to audition for this show without you buddy.* I was going to call my parents but then that would mean making an extra stop to double back and pick them up. At that point, the girls and I had already talked about them auditioning because there were parts for children. They selected a song and had their own sheet music.

We get there and it is a serious audition. I noticed other kids but they were older and everyone seemed to know each other. Then I realized that the show takes place on a boat and they did have an age requirement which meant technically Tasha was too young, but she was rehearsing her song all week. What am I going to tell her now that I know she is too young? I looked at the crowd and the girls changed into their dance shoes. Maybe I should confirm with the girls if they still want to audition. Jasmin was a yes. Traci was a no. Tasha was a yes. I actually needed a yes, yes, and a no from Tasha. So I went up and we went through the jazz portion of the routine. I couldn't believe how fast they taught this and how fast these other girls were catching on. I hadn't danced in 12 years and I was trying to hang with women who looked like they just did a damn show yesterday. Well, that was not far from the truth as several of them had just wrapped a show a few weeks prior. So in essence, I'm trying to hang with the pros. I gave it my best.

Then they took a break and we went over to the singing auditions. Jasmin had finally convinced Traci to go through with it. So they went up individually and handed the pianist their music and climbed up on the stage. They walked to the center, introduced themselves, and they stated the song they were going to sing. They bowed, gathered their music and waited for each one to finish. Jasmin told Traci that she was proud of her and gave her a high five. The judges just watched their whole interaction transpire and were blown away by their behavior, manners, and how they were supporting each other.

When they walked back to their seat Tasha asked when she was going to go. I said, "Well maybe they made a mistake. Let me go talk to the people." I knew I was going to have to fix this somehow. I went up to the judges and said that I didn't realize there was an age limit for the show and that my youngest has a song she has been preparing to sing all week and if they would allow her to audition as well. I could see they were a family-friendly group and very supportive of one another. The worst that they could do was say "no". They responded, "Sure!" Thank God for that.

I ran back down the aisle and told Tasha that I didn't realize she may be too young for the show, but that they would like her to audition. She grabbed her music, walked down the aisle, and handed her Barney Song to the pianist. She couldn't get her foot to the top step on the side of the stage. One of the kids up front helped her and told her where to stand. The auditorium immediately got quiet and all eyes were on her. She introduced herself and her song. The pianist asked if she was ready, she said "Okay," and began to sing.

After she finished, the judges and everyone stood up and applauded. She was grinning from ear to ear in her little dress with her clickity shoes. They watched her walk down the aisle and back to her seat. The three girls were complimenting each other on their audition. It was explained to all of the children performers that they would be informed after the second day of auditions on who made the show. Tasha grabbed her coat said she was tired and put her head down.

They announced it's time for the tap portion. I was so proud of their performances. It was a true proud mommy moment. I knew nothing about the musical itself and based on what I'd seen, I didn't think they were old enough for the roles, but they auditioned for a real theater group, so I was tickled pink.

Most of the dancers were already on stage and finding their spot. I wanted to be in the back. Oh my God. I thought the jazz portion of the dance was taught fast and then the tap was added in double time, then there were formation changes. I made it through the first set. I remembered the dance moves but didn't remember the full choreography. They announced a break. I could see that my girls were tired and they had school the next day. They called us back to the stage to try another tap routine. I was getting it and then I could see all of the girls' heads were down. It was actually too late for them to be out, so during one of the next breaks I gathered the girls and my things and decided I had done my best. I sang my audition song, I tap danced and did a jazz routine with a little acting. I was good. I called it quits and headed home.

I was very pleased with my audition and knew that since I walked out I eliminated myself. But in my heart, I had to be a mommy at that moment and do what was best for my girls. There will be other auditions now that I know where to look. The good thing was that several of the talents work in schools, so they know we have activities like parent-teacher conferences, back to school, and events, so our availability changes.

The next evening my phone rang. It was Barbie from Mystic Vision Players. She talked about the competition during the audition and how everyone was so talented. She said that they were looking for me after the audition and realized I was gone. I shared with her that my girls were tired and I wasn't catching on to the choreography at that pace. I told her that if that was going to be how things were taught, then I might as well quit while I'm ahead, so I went home.

Barbie explained that was the pace to just to get through the audition and that they take out more time to teach when you make the show. She shared what they thought about my audition and asked me to join the cast. I was shocked, but I remained calm. We reviewed my availability and she gave me more information about the rehearsals and show dates. Then she talked about the girls and shared that they were looking for kids with a little more acting experience. But she added that my girls were the talk of the casting meeting, especially that little one. We had a family meeting and I shared the casting feedback with the girls. While they were disappointed, they saw that the other kids had more experience, so they understood. Even the kids at the audition had just done a previous show. I was still in shock that they could actually see the old girl still had it with this tapping thing. I just needed a bit of a slower pace on the teaching side.

After the call, I pulled out that rehearsal calendar. OH MY Goodness! I was truly on my own trying to figure out how to do this show and run around with the girls. I had already been a planning queen, so I was putting the pieces of this puzzle together. Gary saw my commitment to this and he began to see that I could make it work without him. He stopped giving me such a hard time and began to help. Before I knew it, we were wrapping up after two weekends of six shows and the theater bug hit me hard. I was excited hearing about plans for the next show, *American Rapture*. It was a rock and roll soul review with top hits from the '50s, '60s, and '70s. I did that show and loved it. I watched all of the family relationships within the group and was set on asking my Dad to audition. I brought my Dad in. He loved the group and they loved him. The year after that the girls were a little older and we did their Christmas performance at a local church. This group was always very welcoming and fun to be around. I still never got to that liberating comfort level of just being the free spirit I wanted to be.

My thoughts still go back to, *How did I go from loud Joi on the playground, to being so shy and introverted. I get on my own nerves! What in the world am I afraid of?* When I was acting and performing, it is just that. It doesn't mean that's who you are. This is what made me realize that although I have a gift for singing and dancing, it's not the gift that God has intended for my life. I think if it was, then I would be that person who just sings anywhere and doesn't care who's listening.

I enjoyed the moment and used the stage to help me open up a little more and translate over into how I interact with people socially. Before becoming a mother I had always read that our fears and anxieties can be magnified in our children when they watch our actions. So as I mentioned earlier, there were certain things that I definitely didn't want for my children, so I forced them to be social. My thoughts went back to how my girls were talking to everyone during rehearsals. Again, I never wanted them to pick up my social anxieties.

To be honest, Jasmin got so bad with taking over conversations that people didn't think Traci could talk. Jasmin was always taking the lead and introducing everyone. She was the organizer and this translated into her life as she got older and she became the life of the party because she always had a plan for everyone's events. While we never really got into doing other shows, it is something that I still want to do. Especially now that I know it's in my gene pool. I also want us to step out an do a family album combining *all* the vocalists and musicians on all sides of my family. I'm so excited. We are getting it done in the next two years and I'm expecting @HeyTasha3 and @JSpizzy to produce an original for us, @OlliesHairSalon to give us those precision cuts, @ TangibleTresses @StudioShiShi to handle all the natural hair care, @ allthingsafrocentric to design some fly Afrocentric garments. I also hope to find someone to teach me about makeup and posing so we can have professional photographs and make this a memorable occasion. I'm claiming this one. *Who run the world? Girls*!

14

As the Girls Turn

Candid Conversations

In May 2015, I received a call from my close friend Gwynetta regarding the passing of someone near and dear to my entire family, Ms. Bettie Quinn. Ms. Quinn was an educator and administrator in the Plainfield school system for decades. She was my mentor and friend early in my career. When I heard the news all I could think of were the great times we had at Jefferson School, Hubbard Middle School, the parties at her house, great wine, laughter, and her wonderful family. I actually saw myself dancing with her at her birthday party and hearing her infectious laugh. Nothing compared to her split pea soup in the winter and the delicious meals she cooked for me when I was in graduate school. Not only that, Ms. Quinn and Ms. Middleton gave me class coverage during my college final exams in my last semester in school. She gave a speech at our sorority event for Delta Sigma Theta Women of Achievement when we celebrated her lifetime achievements and contributions to the children in Plainfield. All I can say is that Ms. Quinn gave plenty of love to all who she came in contact with. So how was I going to tell the girls that she was gone?

I decided to tell my two older girls Jasmin and Traci first. Tasha might not be able to handle it at that moment. I didn't want them to read about it on social media before I told them. We were all in the kitchen while Jasmin was preparing dinner. I needed to get Tasha out of the room.

"Tasha "Do you have homework?"

"Yes, I do."

"OK I will talk to your sisters and then you and I will talk after you finish your homework."

I make eye contact with Traci and repeat that I need to talk to her and Jasmin. Tasha heard me when she got to the top of the steps and yelled, "She's Pregnant!" Jasmin said, "You're late nights."

Tasha continues yelling from upstairs, "She's Pregnant! She's Pregnant!"

"What's wrong mom?" Traci asked.

Tasha yelled again, "She's Pregnant Tra. She's Pregnant! It's a Miracle. This is a wonder baby. He's going to the Pros!"

Is she serious? What the heck would make them think I'm pregnant? I'm not trying to have any kids.

After the shock wears off, I tell them "Relax! Tasha. That's not it at all. I am not pregnant. I AM NOT PREGNANT! I can't believe this. Yall have issues. Pregnant? Really?"

By now, Traci was getting antsy and nervous walking back and forth trying to stare through me. Jasmin is still cooking with her back to both of us.

"Go ahead mom, I'm listening. I just don't want this food to burn," Jasmin stated.

"Ms. Quinn died today."

Traci's mouth dropped open and she held her heart. Jasmin was still moving around in the kitchen and was not as responsive. Traci's eyes started to water. Jasmin just stopped moving. My mind was racing with thoughts of them with Bettie Quinn and all of our moments with her over many years. My heart ached. I don't want to think too much. My friends did not want to call me because they knew I had my hands full with my husband and the separation, and all that drama. My plate was full and I was already an emotional wreck. I was upset that I didn't get to see her before she passed; that sat with me for a long time. My friends told me Quinn was happy to see them but also not happy to see them. She fussed at them for seeing her like that in the hospital. I figured she was still fighting cancer and I had time. Quinn and I usually communicated via text message and she hadn't responded to my message three weeks prior, so I wasn't sure what was going on.

Sitting there made me think of the old saying about the law of three in death. You never hear about just one, for some reason, death tends to come in threes. I immediately thought of my step-father, Maurice, who was in the hospital and I knew I had to go visit him. After Ms. Quinn's loss, Traci would want to see Maurice as well. Tasha is kind of a wild card. She doesn't like to deal with death or sick people. Jasmin would not want to see Maurice in the hospital either. He wouldn't want us to see him in that capacity as well. I don't like visiting people in the hospital. I don't know what to do in those quiet moments, the small talk, or those awkward situations; how long do I stay? When do I leave? The news of Quinn's death brings a stillness over the house and we all just sit there for a moment in silence.

Although I know prayer works, I needed something to calm my mind. I began meditating each night. I sent away for meditation CDs and I realized that I was supposed to get another CD for free but it never came. I emailed the contact and received an immediate response. I had been using the tracks wrong. One side was informational and the other side was the meditation exercises. Finding a way to remain calm and be strong for my girls was my priority.

I often share relatable stories with my students to help them see that I was really a teenager and that what they are doing or experiencing is nothing new. So I told Traci, my middle daughter, my theory about sharing my stories with the three of them because I did not want one of my students to know something about me that I never told either of my own children. Before I could finish my thought, Traci took the opportunity to ask every question she could think of.

"Sooo have you ever smoked marijuana?"

"Yep, not looking at her."

"A lot, a little, a few times… How old were you."

"Middle school."

"Middle school! WHAT? Where did you get it?"

"I can't tell you that."

"So you know how to roll?"

"No, it was already rolled."

She smiled and said, "I was gonna say, Mommy can roll a joint. Can I tell my sisters this story?"

"No, this is exactly why I have to tell you *all* at the same time, my story doesn't get messed up or mixed up as you all try to interpret it"

"Well, we gotta do this soon. So I guess at least I can say, "Well my mommy smoked in Middle School.""

"It's not your story to tell! You can't say anything. And it was only once or twice by the way. That weed I found was old and horrible."

This is why I have a fear of telling my girls my story. I did some dumb stuff at all different ages; when I was younger than them and older than them. I don't want them to confuse my actions with my consent to do dumb things. As educators and adults, I think it's because of the dumb stuff that we did in our youth, makes us better equipped to help our students. We've been there, done that.

Tattoos

It was during Thanksgiving 2015, that it sunk in for the first time; the family I longed for and tried to maintain for years would never be the same. The girls had been talking about getting tattoos and then we talked about doing something important to get our minds off the holiday stuff. Jasmin had already had a few tattoos. Traci was ready to get her first ink. I always wanted a tattoo, but never anything without meaning. So Traci found this meaning of an arrow tattoo. The meaning spoke of when life pulls you back, know that you will always push forward and soar. So as she shared this, I thought about the arrow being pulled back was a great concept then I realized an arrow plummets to the ground very quickly, so I said I would think about it.

When we arrived at the tattoo parlor I still wasn't sure I was going to do. I already knew Traci was getting a tattoo and Jasmin was going to get one as well. The girls began talking about making this a family event. So Tasha started asking about getting a tattoo as well. I'm thinking, yes, *we were looking for something to do, but who in the world would think on Thanksgiving, let's go get tattoos! Talk about crazy! Who would think that I would take my girls to a tattoo parlor?* While we were moving forward, they were talking and I'm just walking into the place. Then I made an about face and started walking back to the car. *What am I thinking?* Jasmin and Traci were like, *Well we are here now. Traci is getting her tattoo, so either way, we need to go into the place.* They looked through the books I sat in the front area as Jasmin talked to the guy at the counter. Some young kids walked in at first I thought they were my students. Then, I realize that they are drunk in preparation for their tattoo. No, I'd say two of them had been drinking. The other at least was the driver and he appeared sober. I always heard stories about drunk people getting a tattoo they regret. *Do I really need alcohol for the pain? My family unit is no more. Thanksgiving is a family day. I'm sitting in a tattoo parlor. What's this design Traci is talking about? What does it mean?*

Everything seemed just like an out-of-body experience. Although I knew where we were and what we were talking about doing, it really wasn't hitting home. The permanency of what we were about to do did not surface. So the girls picked out their tattoo and I decided at the last minute that if an arrow plummeting to the Earth after being pulled back happens that would not be good. Then I thought that my arrow should be on the side of my arm and that it has to be in the shape of an infinity sign. It turns out, Jasmin and Traci wanted the straight arrow. Tasha and I got the same infinity arrow. It got to the point where Tasha was asking me where should she get it and then she changed her mind about getting it a few times. I looked around to take it all in again. I was staring at the back wall thinking, *it's Thanksgiving and I'm sitting in a tattoo parlor with my three girls about to get tattoos.*

We finalized our designs and the location. I decided that I wanted the design on my wrist. I thought the wrist wouldn't be as visible, but it would still be in a spot that could be covered. Tasha wanted hers on the right outside part of her upper arm. Jasmin came over to me and took my credit card. She waved me over to come and sign. She told me that I had to sign a waiver because Tasha was 16. At one point Tasha was in the back just yelling. It turned out that the guy didn't even put the needle on her arm yet. She came out to the front and her mouth was moving. She tapped me and said, "I think I changed my mind again."

"WAIT did you hear me yelling?"

I looked at her and did not answer, *HUH, girl I just paid for this but if you don't want to, fine.*

Then she said, "No, I'm going to go through with it because all of us were going to get it and we said we'd do it together."

Jasmin said, "Mommy you really didn't hear her yelling? You know the guy didn't even touch her with the thing he just turned it on."

The whole time I was still in a fog. We all got tattoos. A few days later I realized that while I made sure that my tattoo was in a spot that could easily be covered, I don't know what I was thinking when I let Tasha get her tattoo on her forearm. OH MY GOODNESS it's going to show if she wears ANYTHING sleeveless. ON HER FOREARM. *Joi, what were you thinking?* The girls echoed, "We had these things for three days already and now you are just realizing where she put her tattoo?" I always wanted one, but I let Tasha get a tattoo at 16 years of age on her forearm for all the world to see. She's got the prom, she's got track. *OH MY GOODNESS. I did WHAT? I let her do WHAT? What does this thing mean again? Thanksgiving tattoo. SMH.*

The girls and I always sit and laugh about how much I was in a daze at that tattoo parlor. The fact that Tasha cried the entire time and was crying *before* the guy even touched her with a needle was comical. The older two girls have a straight arrow. It's long and huge. Tasha and I have the infinity arrow. I didn't realize how much that made her stand out. Now that I think about it, her sleeveless track tank tops already showed her tattoo. She can honestly say, "yes, my mom knows I have the tattoo, she actually has the same one." This thought alone is quite hilarious.

Now around Thanksgiving, they text each other to make this an annual thing. Oddly enough the next year we all got another one. The year after that, I must admit I went back and got butterflies. The butterfly symbolizes the struggles that the butterfly goes through before it actually becomes a butterfly. The output in a struggle is not easy for the life of the butterfly. Yet while the butterfly is struggling, it is developing strength, stamina, and releasing fluids from the body that help it move and become beautiful. I have three butterflies on my shoulder. Three has been a special number not only for the number of children that I have, but three represents the past, present, and future. When I got married, I had three bridesmaids: an old friend, a new friend and a relative. I've learned that the number three plays an important part in our family history.

Although I'm not planning another Thanksgiving tattoo parlor trip, I tell my girls that I don't think I want another one. Yet in the back of my mind there are a couple of other tattoos that I really might like having. My thoughts range from a triangle for adoption because it also represents my sorority, Delta Sigma Theta. I've got this thing with hearts. I know that one day I'm going to find true love and it's something about hearts that make me smile and that symbol is also connected to the adoption symbol. The other day, I received an announcement with hearts and I saw a potential tattoo brewing. I want to find love that doesn't hurt. I saw a tattoo with love written in cursive on the inside of the ring finger or it could be something on the other side of my wrist or something on my ankle.

People who notice the tattoo on my wrist always ask what is the meaning of the infinity symbol tattoo. The story seems to be the same wherever I've read it. The **infinity** symbol is a never-ending loop. So, it **means** forever or always or limitless, never-ending possibilities. It is a positive tattoo. When you combine my arrow of being pulled back and then being launched into greatness with a never-ending loop, for me, it means anything and everything that tries to pull me back will get the opposite reaction. After I launch, I'm headed toward a never-ending loop of possibilities. I think that pretty much sums up my future.

Why an Arrow Tattoo?

I shared with Rodney, cousin Pat's husband my elevator speech on why we all got arrow tattoos. A few days after our discussion he sent me a message with another description of the meaning of an arrow in a poem, "On Children," by Kahil Gibran.

On Children

Your children are not your children.
They are the sons and daughters of Life's longing for itself.
They come through you but not from you,
And though they are with you yet they belong not to you.

You may give them your love but not your thoughts,
For they have their own thoughts.
You may house their bodies but not their souls,
For their souls dwell in the house of tomorrow,
which you cannot visit, not even in your dreams.
You may strive to be like them,
but seek not to make them like you.
For life goes not backward nor tarries with yesterday.

You are the bows from which your children
as living arrows are sent forth.
The archer sees the mark upon the path of the infinite,
and He bends you with His might
that His arrows may go swift and far.
Let your bending in the archer's hand be for gladness;
For even as He loves the arrow that flies,
so He loves also the bow that is stable.
- **Khalil Gibran**

LESSON THREE

THE JOY OF EDUCATION

15

A Song for Education

"Education will be seriously reformed only after we move it from a matter of "importance" to a matter of "life and death," both for society and for the individuals themselves."
- ***Martin Haberman***

The courses that I have taken and the experiences of the past four years at Kean University made me realize the importance of getting all stakeholders to respond with deliberate speed to identify and address the needs of the students we serve. I've read a great deal on Haberman and he states that high school graduates with limited information and just basic skills are dangerous. We are living in dangerous times. In times like these, leadership in schools has become a tremendous task.

I've worked hard to be a great leader. When defining my leadership philosophy I often compare it to my love of music. When I worked in various roles in the Union County and Middlesex County School Districts, I strived to define the skill sets that a graduate from middle school and high school must possess. As my colleagues and I worked to create a list, we also identified the types of support that students will need, and resources the staff needs as well as the needs of all stakeholders involved to attain those goals.

I began to view this high school graduate like a song being sung by a choir. Within a choir there are sopranos, altos, tenors and bass voices. Each singer must know their notes, melodies, rhythms, and must have the ability to blend with those in their voice part, while also tuning in to those around them in the other sections. I believe we need to approach educational stakeholders with this same segmentation of expertise. We must all clarify and understand our roles in the schools. The school district staff, the school staff, parents, community, the board, and students, must all be aware of their role in producing a skilled graduate or like in music, keeping a beautiful song on key.

There's nothing more exciting to me than to sing in a group where the harmony is so tight, you hear a hum as if an instrument is playing. To get a group to that perfect pitch sound, each voice part must be completely in tune with the other. Each voice part must concentrate on reading and studying their role and responsibility. Each person must understand the melody and be very clear with their notes. This humming sound I refer to cannot be achieved if one voice is slightly off.

Achieving this harmony means that each individual must take the necessary steps to ensure they understand their role. It takes teamwork, patience, practice, encouragement, great listening, and a commitment to learning your role to reach that hum. One of the other joys is that even if the hum isn't achieved from the perfect harmony, we can still make mistakes along the way, practice hard, and ultimately end up with a great song.

It is through that same determination, drive and fine-tuning that we must approach what goes on in our schools. As educational leaders, we must listen, we must have a vision (or song) to work from and the group must practice (staff development). There must be a commitment on the part of each stakeholder to learn their role and how it impacts the song (student achievement). We may not reach perfect harmony but we must strive to at least sing the same song.

16

Things They Don't Teach in School

I wasn't an education major in college, so in my early years in the field I used to think, *I guess I missed this since I wasn't an education major.* I always took it upon myself to take classes and attend workshops. After over 20 years in this field, I can honestly say there are one thousand and one things they don't teach in an education class. I've completed my Masters in Educational Supervision, and I can say my day to day interactions with students, staff, families, and the community, present things that I was never taught in ANY class.

For the most part, I can't even talk about this stuff at home or really to anyone I know because this craziness is often unbelievable. And parents who think they understand education are the ones I really can't talk to because people have no idea what goes on behind the doors of a school. Most parents have no clue what their kids say and do even at the middle school level. At the high school level, it is often incomprehensible. Yet I am in disbelief when people outright tell me or my staff that we are making this stuff up! I think of a few of the stories shared here can be turned into, *What Would You Do*, questions for those daring to enter into the field of education.

Now that my daughter Jasmin is part of the third generation of educators in our family, I think it's important for me to share some stuff with her. She has finally realized that she can't resist her gift or the fact that she loves kids and teaching. I'm hoping these scenarios can spark thoughtful conversation.

The Spice of Life or Death

I walked into school one morning and I heard someone say the word "cinnamon." I thought it was odd, but they could've have been talking about the spice. Around midday, I got a call on the radio that about 15 students were in the hall and someone had a bowl of cinnamon. They revealed the name of one student in particular. In the meantime, our security officers brought in three students who were caught in the melee. The students were asked to write their statements. I spoke to them briefly and learned that they were involved in something called The Cinnamon Challenge.

The goal is to place a spoonful of cinnamon on your tongue and hold it in your mouth for as long as you can. The cinnamon begins to burn and then you spit it out. You might throw up as well. Then I learned that several of my students *may* have bottles of cinnamon. Here's where the education class experience should kick in right? Wrong! Nobody taught me anything about this group of social media challenge mess. So, I think back to what would G do? No, not God. G was the first administrator I worked under in a chaotic middle school just three years ago.

G would pull the school or grade together in a heartbeat and just "go off." But it was close to lunch and that would totally interrupt the day. I went to my office to think and decided I'd better check this out on YouTube. After which I called in the security team and the school nurse to view what I found. A 100% check of the school would take way too long. So I thought we could do a security drill to gather everyone.

Due to the health risks, I decided that the Cinnamon Challenge was important enough to interrupt the school day. So today was the day I was going to lecture them, make them feel as if they disappointed me, and alarm them of the health risks. My goal was to convince someone by the end of my talk to turn over their cinnamon bottles, cups, spoons or whatever they had to perform this silly and deadly challenge. I didn't want this mess landing any student in the hospital on my watch.

I called the drill. We gathered in our shelter location and I opened with my dramatic presentation bull horn in hand because I didn't have time to get the sound system set up. I told them that there was something very serious to talk about. I needed them to understand that some of the decisions they made could have serious implications for their health. I told them that when I came to the school in September I never came with the goal of attending a student funeral.

By now they were looking at me like I was crazy. I kept going with the fact that the teachers don't want to attend a student or several students funerals and I'm sure none of them want to attend a funeral of a classmate, especially when they have a chance to save a life and make a better choice. I asked who heard of the Cinnamon Challenge. The kids were seated by grade level so I could see one-third of the eighth grade and one-fifth of the seventh grade raised their hands. I then turned to the staff and asked how many of them have heard of this challenge. Not one hand went up.

I asked the kids to describe this "game." They went on to say that you put cinnamon in your mouth and try to swallow it. Then some were saying some things that were way off. So I took them through what it meant. I was concerned about telling them how to do it, but my counter-punch was that I would let the nurse scare them with the possible outcomes. So I explained that someone may ask or has already asked them to put a spoonful of cinnamon on their tongue to time how long they can hold it in their mouth to be middle school, Cinnamon Challenge Winner. If that were the case, then they needed to know the risks. I asked them if they realized that to win they could damage their esophagus and damage their lungs. Before I went any further and screwed up my message about the respiratory system, I handed the megaphone to the nurse.

She explained to them that as they spit out the cinnamon, at the same time, they are inhaling it, which burns their esophagus. Now, they have cinnamon in their lungs. She shared that cinnamon in their lungs becomes particles that don't absorb into the lungs and that this can impact their breathing. The nurse told them that they may experience a cold-like cough and other breathing symptoms. She shared that we needed to know who to look out for over the coming weeks so it would be very important that those who have cinnamon come forward. I announced that leniency would be granted to those who willingly turned it in. They could even turn it in for a friend and I'd accept it. The nurse also reinforced the fact that we would need to inform the parents of those students who tried it for health reasons.

At the close of the meeting, I reminded them that if they saw or heard something they wouldn't want a friend to leave school today and wind up passed out somewhere with a breathing issue. Before I could get out of the gym, a young man stated that he needed to talk to me for his friend. I tried to get him to wait for the crowd to leave, but he didn't care. He wanted to share his story and make sure his friend could remain anonymous. So he told me his story and as we were headed to my office, he said, "Never mind." I looked at him kind of shocked. Across the hall, we saw his friend sitting in the room with security and a bottle of cinnamon in his hand. He said. "Looks like it's taken care of already." The pattern that he told me involved two brothers who were always in trouble with him, and where one is, the other isn't far behind doing something crazier.

Turns out, the older brother was bringing in his younger brother's bottle of cinnamon on his behalf. Little did he know that his younger brother had already given a bottle of cinnamon to the teacher across the hall following our "assembly." So when the teacher brought me the bottle and said his name, I said, "his brother just gave me a bottle that he said was his. I called in the younger brother who confessed and talked about how cool things looked on YouTube. He confessed to having a small container of cinnamon but not the bottle. He was surprised to hear that his brother said the bottle belonged to him.

"Why do you think your big bro would set you up?" I asked.

"Because I'm the one who always gets in trouble. He doesn't want my parents to think he does anything bad, so he knew that they would expect it to be from me and then he wouldn't get in any trouble. I know how he thinks, but that bottle ain't mine, I brought the bowl!"

At this point, all I could do was chuckle. I reinforced my disappointment and need to know who might have really ingested the cinnamon. Before the day was over we had three containers of cinnamon.

We learned that the Facebook message had been circulating for two days. The message was for kids to bring it to school today and meet during the third period. A separate group of boys and girls in neighboring bathrooms were to be videotaped for YouTube. We learned that three schools were involved. With that said, we began our investigation and learned who tried it, who said they would try it, who forwarded the Facebook message, who showed up in the bathroom, who almost threw up, who was going to try it after school, and more details. I emailed my colleagues from the other schools and the superintendent.

As our day went on, I received messages about the number of students who ran out of class or to the garbage can earlier in the day because they were sick. Now that people were armed with information we began to put many pieces to the puzzle together. Of all the people involved only two of the thirty plus students denied that they knew anything about it. It turns out it was the two brothers who started the Facebook forwards. Unfortunately, for them, their nicknames on Facebook were recognizable by all even without a picture.

Parents of the kids who ingested the cinnamon were called. Students gave up the names. Other schools were notified and I sent out a letter to go home to parents. How do you explain this nonsense?

Fire Flow

Two young men were brought into the office first thing in the morning. They were lighting smoke bombs in front of the school. Then they use the lighter to set the tree on fire. When I spoke with them, the first boy said, "Oh no, Ms. Fisher, I wasn't trying to set the tree on fire. I wanted to see how the smoke flowed through the bark of the tree and up into the air."

"Are you kidding me? Please tell me whose bright idea this was?

"What do you mean by that?" he inquired.

"Tell me which one of your friends thought this was something wise or smart to do? "

"Well, I wanted to see what would happen when we lit it."

In between the questioning, I learned that they lit three smoke bombs and got the lighter from someone else who they told 'We need a lighter to light these smoke bombs'.

"Okay, so now they all know you are about to do something wrong and they gave it to you." Then he lit the smoke bomb, and the staff thought the building was on fire. Panic ensued and we had two of the boys who ended up in the office.

I asked, "Could you identify the kid who gave you the lighter?" They knew the class he had for homeroom and first period, but no one knew his name. So I sent them with security to find this kid. They all came back and I had security go outside to retrieve the evidence. Security found three paper Mache-looking cardboard balls with what appeared to be a gunpowder substance and a lighter at the bottom of the tree. So while the boys were writing statements, I logged into YouTube and pulled up a video on smoke bombs. I learned that one smoke bomb can fill several classrooms with smoke. I saved this video as evidence.

When we contacted parents, one of the parents insisted that it was not their child who brought it in. The child of the parent who argued the most was the child who admitted to bringing it to school, but he said they lit the bomb far away from the school when in reality he did it on school grounds because he wanted his friends to see what would happen. The boys received a long-term suspension and had to have a superintendent's hearing to return. School safety is critically important. Smoke bombs were never taught in any of my classes. I don't think we will ever be able to keep up with the nonsense on YouTube that instantly captures these kids' attention.

Stairway to Change

Andrew was as bad as hell. He was always doing something to cause trouble. So his math teacher and I decided to do a home visit during dinner time. They lived on the second floor of a home around the corner from the school. When we walked up to the house we realized there had to be 50 stairs to get to the front door.

We stopped in about 6:00 PM because we hadn't been able to reach mom. His family was at the table preparing to eat dinner. We shared Andrew's antics with his mom. We talked about his incomplete work, his failing grades, his detentions, his behavior with all of his peers and everything we could think of. Then we mentioned that he knew the phones were disconnected, so for the past few weeks he was really showing out. His math teacher spoke directly to him and told him that he needed to take his grades seriously and modify his behavior. His mom reassured us that he would get it together and she provided us with an updated phone number. Andrew did not like that.

The impact of visiting Andrew at home was more profound than we ever imagined. Apparently, the next day he told everybody in my homeroom and her homeroom that when we say "We'll be by during dinner" that we will do it! This story spread and lived on as part of our reputation for the 11 years I was at that school. The math teacher and I were known to be people who would show up at your house if you didn't get it together. I learned my lesson about home visits. The following week after our visit, I drove by the house and saw that the house was condemned and the stairs collapsed. I never did another home visit.

17

A Call to Do Better

I have been a youth advocate for over 20 years. Now that I am no longer in the teaching capacity in the classroom, I try to use every opportunity I have to encourage and empower educators to do more and make a lasting impact on the next generation. I was honored to speak to a group of educators at the annual Convocation Ceremony:

I'd first like to thank Ms. Belin Pyles, members of our Board, and the team of coordinators for inviting me to speak. My name is Joi Fisher and I am the Acting Principal at Maxson Middle School.

- ☐ *I stand before you as someone who comes from a long line of educators: my father was a teacher/administrator, my uncle has his doctorate in education, two other uncles were educators, and another uncle taught BUT in a prison setting. The last thing I wanted to become was a teacher. I worked every summer while in middle school at a summer camp. Teaching, NOT FOR ME!! Or so I thought.*
- ☐ *I am also a graduate of PHS Class of 1975 pre-K-program and a graduate of Emerson, Maxson, and PHS*
- ☐ *I stand before you as a former honor roll student who had no aspirations of going to college. And as a student who memorized everything she needed to know for tests through 12th grade.*
- ☐ *I stand before you as a student who had to take remedial college courses and as a student who had no clue how to study once she got to college.*

Not a bad kid in school, very active in activities, freshman and Se-

nior Class President. Played soccer, basketball and ran track, friendly but very little confidence in knowing what my skill set was. My experience isn't unique, but it is one we have the ability to change. This didn't mean I wasn't smart-this didn't mean I couldn't go on to college. I had gaps in my learning. I earned my Bachelor's degree in Criminal Justice. I graduated with a Master's degree in Educational Leadership with a 3.9 GPA and am now currently a doctoral candidate at Rowan University, and I know the possibilities for our students are endless.

We have the best and the brightest educators. We have the most dedicated administrators and support staff. We have children who are willing to learn. Parents who want a good education for their children, and a community who wants to support us. Now is the time to pull all the pieces together.

We know that our educational climate and parental involvement has to improve our response to gangs and bullying is going to make or break us. Holding ON to best practices instead of being married to programs is going to make or break us. Our response to providing engaging lessons that have real-life connections are going to make or break us. Our use of data to drive instruction and our response to providing on-going professional development for new programs is going to make or break us. Our response to recruiting and maintaining quality educators and connecting with the local universities is going to make or break us, our use of technology in the classroom is going to make or break us and our response to collaborating on OUR issues is going to make or break us. These things are challenges but also opportunities.

Our parents are sending us the best children they have, so while we have them we have to do what is necessary for them to succeed. And we have stories of success. WE have children in the 300 club for perfect NJ ASK scores, we have college students on the Dean's list, graduates who are professors, graduates leading successful military careers, entrepreneurs, lawyers, actors, doctors, police officers, accountants, firefighters, nurses, those returning to our schools as substitutes and teachers, we have many students on the right path, many parents who support us and many community businesses stepping in.

So today, I challenge you to take a child under your wing, take a

Joi R. Fisher

staff member under your wing, encourage a parent to come and get involved, provide extra support to someone in need, make a positive phone call, join a committee, encourage someone to think about obtaining a degree to develop a gift you see in them, honestly REFLECT on what your commitment is to the school and to the district. This work will take our collective effort, ongoing and honest communication, some tough conversations or "real talk", some decisions that may not be in the best interest of your school, but be the best interest for the district. The work that needs to be done is not impossible.

Our Superintendent recently shared at a board meeting that this isn't about a blame game. WE all bear some responsibility. And we all must step up our game. When I accepted the role of Acting Principal my response to the team after the "WOW was I accept the CHALLENGE but I will need support." So as we enter the new school year I ask you "Do you accept the challenge? Are you willing to seek the support you need? Are you willing to support what is in the best interest of the district? Are you willing to share your stories of struggle and triumph? Are you prepared to make a difference in the life of a child? What are you willing to do to ensure our children are learning? Our motto says no alibis, no excuses no exceptions. So this girl from Plainfield asks on behalf of all the children-Do YOU accept the challenge?

In closing, my daughter came home a couple of years ago with this chant her Spanish teacher Mr. Bateman wrote and I wanted to share it with you...Repeat after me:

You can do it if you think you can.
Work hard, stay focused, and believe you can.
Don't give up, don't miss your chance (say) – Si say
Puede.

(Stomp, Clap, Slap thigh)

126

LESSON FOUR

THE JOY OF CONNECTION

18

80 Questions

As an adoptee, no matter how old you are, questions about your birth parents are never-ending. Every day I think of another question that I want to ask my birth mom and I just keep adding to my list. It's been over a year since our reunion and I'm too afraid to bombard her with all of my questions. I make small talk to try to find answers to as many on my list. So far, I still have more questions. It's hard. I feel guilty sometimes because I want to give Flo the third degree. *Why don't I feel as angry with my dad? It's as if he gets a pass because he is a man.* It could be a subconscious thing. I'm not sure.

I was born April 7, 1970, so I initially narrowed my list down to 70 questions. Then there were a few more that I just had to include. I actually have about 170 questions but I will stop at 80 for now. I hope our communication grows organically, and eventually, I will have answers. Now I know where my daughter Traci gets her incessant questioning from. It's definitely genetic.

Dear Flo,

1. You made sure I was given life, why?
2. My non-identifying information mentioned that my birth father knew you were going through this. Did you at least discuss it with him first?
3. You mentioned in the information being alone. There was no one you could turn to?
4. Are you tall? I'm tall so I always assumed you were tall.
5. Do you know that I fantasized about seeing someone who looked like me in a magazine?

6. I've always known that I was adopted. My mother ALWAYS made sure I knew that you had an adoption plan for my best interest. After all these years, do you think it was in my best interest?

7   What is it that you thought you could not provide?

8. What was your relationship with my father?

9. How did you meet my father?

10. How long before meeting him did you get pregnant?

11. When did you find out you were pregnant?

12. How did you break it to him?

13. What was his reaction?

14. What happened the day after you told him?

15. The adoption records say that your parents never knew. Those were the first words I read when I received my non-identifying information. I cried and cried and cried waiting a few days before I could muster the courage to read the rest.

16. Did you go to school in the Trenton area?

17. How did you get to that area?

18. I went to college in Trenton and rode by both hospitals in the early '90s wondering which one I may have been born in. Did you choose the hospital?

19. Did you know where I was for two months prior to placement in foster care?

20. Did you have any input on who adopted me?

21. Did they notify you that I was adopted?

22. After delivery, the nurse usually hands the baby to the mom? Did you hold me or did they immediately take me away?

23. If you held me, what was going through your mind?

24. What was the goodbye like?

25. What were your hopes and dreams for me?

26. I was a straight tomboy growing up. Good athlete. Good in the field of the arts but battled with being too much in the limelight. I desired it and believed I could do it but never wanted to take the risks to get it done. Were you athletic?

27. Are you a lover of the arts?

28. I took piano lessons and had a great ear, but really refused to learn how to read the notes. Where does my musical gift come from? I know I hear things differently than the average person.

29. In middle school and high school, I always had to have a boyfriend. I hated being by myself. Did you always have a boyfriend back then as well?

30. I had a surprising find about my high school sweetheart once we got to college. The entire time we were dating, he had another girl in his life in the city where his grandmother lived. Even after I discovered his cheating, I still couldn't walk away. I was afraid I'd be by myself in college. That sense of betrayal made me connect the thoughts in my mind that if I wasn't good enough for my birth mother, how can I expect any loyalty from anyone else? It didn't matter that my mother always watched out for me (a total Mama Bear I might add) NOT GOOD ENOUGH, NOT GOOD ENOUGH rang loudly in my head often. Did you ever feel you were not good enough?

31. Did you ever find out your boyfriend cheated on you?

32. Going from being well-known in high school with lots of friends to the low end of the totem pole in college, feeling like I wasn't supposed to call home too often, I felt all alone. Not because anyone told me that I couldn't call home, I just didn't. I never felt more homesick or lonely than I did my Freshman year hanging on to a high school sweetheart who really had no interest in a long distance relationship. I think we just didn't know how to break up with one another. Did that ever happen to you?

33. The words NOT GOOD ENOUGH sent me on a spiral that almost lead to my own self-destruction near the end of my Freshman year. I was looking for love in all the wrong places, not caring who I dealt with. I was on a path of self-destruction because I couldn't be by myself. I used alcohol to soothe the pain and to give me the excuse. We've heard it before, "BUT

I was drunk." Don't get me wrong, I drank but realistically, I may have been drunk three times in college. Were you ever drunk? Do you drink?

34. Word got around that folks I had never been with were telling people they were with me. It became, "I slept with who? Did they tell you that? WOW! I wasn't there for that." Fortunately, by my second-semester junior year, life was completely different. Did you have any encounters with guys that you wish never happened?

35. Can you imagine the weirdness/emptiness of what life was like always being aware that you were out there somewhere, but there was never an adult conversation or discussion about you as I got older. I was angry with you but I also figured life could have been much worse if I stayed with you or whatever the story was. Did you have that emptiness wondering what my life was like?

36. For some reason, my birth father was always a second thought. Thoughts of him were never at the forefront of my mind. I prayed that you weren't raped. I prayed that you eventually told someone of my existence so that if I eventually found you, I didn't want it to be an issue. Who did you tell about me?

37. I always wondered if my birth father disappeared or did you distance yourself so that he wasn't involved?

38. Did you ever contact him after I was born?

39. Have you forgiven yourself?

40. I am determined to find you. I was wondering when I do find you, what it's going to be like if you and my birth father have to come in contact with one another?

41. After reading the non-identifying information I didn't get the feeling that my birth father had much say in your decision. Back then I knew if you were pregnant out of wedlock a quick marriage was expected. Was marriage to my birth father an option?

42. Was I the result of a one-night stand? I worried that once I found you he might not believe I was his and it would be yet another denial and another rejection.

43. Since you never told anyone, will you even be open to seeing me? Or will it be here I am but please don't bother me?

44. Will I be able to find out who you are and deal with your not wanting me in your life? I don't think I could handle that rejection. But I just have to find out.

45. Abandonment, Rejection. I will do everything humanly possible not to let people know how I feel about them. When I think I'm letting someone know, I find out that I am not even close to giving them a clue. Am I loveable?

46. As I write this I get angry because I often wondered if I could have been a better me if I knew who I was to begin with. If I knew that I came from a family lineage that was graduating from college in early 1900. If I knew that degrees beyond your masters were EXPECTED. If I knew how smart my family members were. They tried to skip me in Kindergarten but boys bothering me and holding my hand, pulling my braids, made me so uncomfortable, I told them I did not want to stay in first grade and send me back to kindergarten. What were your grades like in school?

47. I was embarrassed to tell my children that I was adopted. I didn't know my nationality, my health history. I moved my baby book every time I rearranged the bookshelf so they wouldn't find it. I never told the girls. We are a big picture-taking family so photo albums were everywhere. I used to hide it within another album. Did you take a baby picture of me at the hospital? Did anyone?

48. My girls found my baby album and the card inside? The album was pretty beat up so I figured they would never look in it. My girls are inquisitive. They ask whatever comes to their mind. I didn't want them asking my parents questions that I never

asked. They then brought me the book and were very upset because they didn't think I knew I was adopted. The older two might have been 11 and 13. Traci was so nervous and unsure how to tell me. Can you imagine what was going through their minds?

49. I know I could never have done what you did. Regardless of the circumstances. I just couldn't do it. Okay, this not not a question, but it was on my mind.

50. You said there are a lot of things that you want to ask me. I've told you that I'm open to it. Is your hesitancy because a conversation is mutual and you know it will be time for you to reveal my adoption story?

51. I never really talked about my adoption story with people because I don't know it. Because it's not a story all my own. Other people's lives are impacted by me just saying "I'm adopted." Did you ever consider the impact it would mean for me to know my story?

52. There was a Sesame Street clip that I hated. They put parents and children and mixed them up and someone then had to try to match up the child and the parent. And I always connected this song. One of these kids .... does not belong. It's a song from childhood.

53. Who has terrible allergies?

54. Who is flat chested (I was just cheated in that department)?

55. Who has a true lack of curves?

56. I never thought I was beautiful. I believed I was cute to my parents because that's what parents are supposed to say. Even as a model, I never thought the real me outside of being glammed up was cute enough. I looked at my body flaws and still thought who would want me? Did you ever wish you looked differently?

57. Did you have any other kids?

58. Did you marry?

59. What's your career?

60. Did you ever try to find me?
61. How will finding me help me come to grips with me?
62. Will a reunion erase or further harm these thoughts that I have about myself?
63. During my marriage, I always felt like I had to keep my marriage together because it was the vow I took. Regardless of how unhappy I was, there was nothing I could do. I wanted to run away. Did you ever feel that way?
64. Anytime there was mention of separation or divorce he threatened that he would never deal with me or "these" kids. For me, those words stung. To say you wouldn't be in your child's life if I didn't stay with you made me feel like I *had* to stay. I didn't want my girls growing up not knowing who their father was. In the end, staying with him was not the answer. I tried to connect all of these dots in my mind.
65. Did you receive money for me?
66. How did you hide your pregnancy? After my birth how did you deal with pregnancy stomach, lactating breast?
67. What triggers did you have as the years moved on? My birthday?
68. Until I was in my 40's I did not know I had a birth name. I know, it not a question.
69. What were your thoughts when you received my letter?
70. What were your greatest fears and worries once I found you?
71. Who did you tell first? Did your sister already know of my existence?
72. Did my cousins ever know or was it news to them?
73. Has Aunt Loretta, your mom's Sister ever asked any further questions after you told her?
74. Do you understand why it is important for me to talk about this? I want to do the adoption panels and share my story but I don't really know how it will bother you and my birth father.
75. Do you understand the magnitude in which this has changed my life?

76. Do you understand how this has opened my heart?
77. Do you know how this has improved my communication with my parents?
78. During one of my therapy sessions doing a mind activity near the end of this visualization, I came across a house. I was asked what I was going to do. I walked up and could only look in the window. Three years later, on the morning I was supposed to meet you, I dreamed I was standing outside that same house. You walked out and walked away from me. I had an anxiety attack the morning we were to meet and I was hesitant if this was something I should go through with for fear of rejection. Did you ever fear my rejection?
79. In sharing my journey, I don't want to say I don't care about how you feel or how my birth father feels, but I can't let any of your fears and inhibitions keep me from doing what I feel God has put on my heart. I can keep you ALL nameless but I have to connect the dots to my life for me. How do you feel about this?
80. Do you have at least this many questions for me?

My Gift of Life

When I think about the things life may have put you through
I believe it must have been a blessing for me not to be with you
Life's little circles has its ups and downs
Children make life hectic if your feet aren't planted firmly in the
ground.

My imagination runs wild when I think of you
Is she tall? Is she thin? Is she a little crazy too?
I get emotional wondering who you could be and what you've been
through

I feel that I need, I need to meet you
To find out if you have thought about me too
No one understands why I feel the way I do
Some days I'm not sure if I want to meet you
BUT every day I wonder how my gift of life has affected you
- Joi R. Fisher

19

Spitting Image Part 2
The First Reunion

Sunday, February 12, 2018

After a few weeks of texting and Facebook messaging, Flo and I agreed to meet at her church for our first face-to-face. I could not sleep for days leading up to Sunday. My mom, dad, Jasmin, Ms. Richardson, Mr. Asante, and my granddaughter Kamryn were with me. When we first got to the church she was in the pulpit, but I couldn't tell if that was even her. A woman was praying on and on so I had time to scan the room. I realized that was Flo, my birth mom in the corner. I was positive once I saw her sister. Even though I couldn't see her face or hair, I was positive it was my birth mom when she stood at the front of the church. She had on an African headpiece for Black History Month. Therefore, with the headpiece and full outfit from head-to-toe, key identifying features were hidden. *Of all days lady, did you really needed to wear that full get up? You're giving me nothing right now!* It was only through her interaction with her sister that I knew it was her. I would have known it was her had I seen the gray hair.

While she stood before the church, I noticed her nose, her mouth, the structure of her jaw and shape of her the mouth caught my eye. The same feelings at that moment aligned with how I felt when I first saw her picture on social media. There was an initial shock when I saw the picture because she looks exactly like my mother! Now that blew my mind. As she moved around upfront, I noticed that she wasn't as big as she looked in some of her Facebook pictures. It was hard to tell her stature because of her clothing.

When I first saw her, I immediately thought of a scene from the movie *Ray,* when he explained to his boys that there was a reason he touched a woman's hand and wrist when he met her. He shared with them that it gave him an indication of her size. Other than her face, I could only see Flo's hands and wrists, I couldn't even see her ankles. I thought, *maybe she's one of those old school preachers that's why she is covered all the way to the floor.* Here I was learning in my late forties to appreciate my stature and my long legs to find that my mom is covered head-to-toe. This was going to be interesting. Lord knows why she has on those boots. They looked like black fishing boots. Then, a light bulb went on in my mind, she did say she had knee surgery.

I thought, *maybe she and my mom can get to know one another and my mom can help her with her attire choices. My mom can go into any store and find a complete outfit that would work for me or my daughters that looks great. She can pick the right size right off the rack. I don't know how she does it but she's got a gift for styling people once she has an idea of a few things that you like. That could be a bonding moment. Enough about the outfit Joi.* Now that Flo was standing and talking, not much about her was registering. I could hear the words but they were in one ear and out the other. As I looked on closely, I couldn't tell if there was anything about her that was like me. I didn't see a match.

I was surprised to see how short she was. My birth mom and her sister are of similar complexion and have gray hair. They wear their hair in a natural salt and pepper afro. When I looked at her Facebook page there were two girls on her page a lot. Prior to meeting my birth mom, my cousin Pat went through her Facebook page. My cousin became familiar with her Facebook page and Pat told me that the two girls all over her page were her nieces, not my sisters. While my hair doesn't look like my birth mom's or my Aunt's, it does looks similar to my cousins. The color of my cousin's hair also looks similar to my natural color.

I noticed Flo wears glasses. I could see the dark circles around her eyes, I naturally have those eyes and they get worse as a reaction to my allergies. I hate wearing my contacts because of these dark circles and I surely can't find a good way to cover them up when wearing makeup. I'm now tuning in to her face. It seemed more appropriate to do this now that she was preaching it gave me a reason to look directly at her.

A few items on the program weren't flowing as planned. Flo made some silly jokes and tried to keep the program moving along. My father leaned across my mom and said, "I see she has a good sense of humor." She was checking in with people throughout the service. She would call for someone to come up and do a part, then learned they were not in church. There were not that many people in the congregation. I'm not sure why things were all out of sorts. This scenario told me that she must have been asked to be the worship leader at the last minute. If this was a last minute notice for her to be the worship leader, why would they do this on this day when she was going to be an emotional wreck? Whose bright idea was this? She seems to be a trooper. She's in it now. Let's see how she handles it. A little chaos and here I was in the flesh sitting in her church and we have yet to speak. This is some made for television Lifetime movie. How is she gonna do under this pressure?

I've learned over the years to let a lot of things that are out of my control just happen. The best thing that I can do in some situations is to try my best to salvage them at the moment. If it falls apart, I've learned to be transparent, honest, laugh about it, and reflect on it later for improvement. You become good at operating on your toes and handling the spur of the moment requests after working with so many school principals. While Flo was fumbling and recovering, I saw a great personality in those mixed-up moments. Her actions and interactions with her sister really made me think of my daughters and their silliness. Or, I'd say it reminded me of the real me that a lot of people don't see unless they're around when we're having our family time; when we relax, chill, and just have fun around the house.

The original plan was for her to give her testimony before her congregation today. Yet before she gave her testimony, there were the regular church protocols that needed to be followed. She introduced the youth, she introduced her sister for the Black History portion of the service, she welcomed the visitors, and then she sang a song. A jack of all trades. Flo was doing everything and her sister had her back with each twist and turn. It was actually fun to watch.

One of the preachers came up and we transitioned into "offering" time. I saw her gathering her papers. Offering meant that the congregation had to walk toward the front of the church to lay their offering in a basket. *Why Lord why? Walking before the church to collect this offering.* At the time I was staying with my Dad because my house was being renovated. I didn't have all of my clothes and shoes. I wasn't happy with my outfit this Sunday. I had to wear my burgundy shoe boots with a black dress that was just long enough to be appropriate for church. *Oh my, I was criticizing Flo's boots and outfit and I had a long dress and clunky boots too!* We all rise and wait for our row to move out. *Do I acknowledge her as I walk up? Do I walk over? Do I wave? Lord, what am I supposed to do?* I walked forward and I glanced over. I dropped in my money and my Dad's money, as he didn't want to walk up. I make my way to my pew. I knew we were getting close to the time for the sermon, maybe she will give her testimony toward the end. *Is she preaching too?* She had her hand in every part of this service so far, why not? She had finally established a comfortable flow. She made her way to the pulpit and began to gather some papers. She appeared very composed.

When she began her testimony, my first thought was, *wow, she writes like me and phrases things like me.* During one particular portion of her testimony, she was talking about the joy of life and the joy of this and the joy of that. Those who didn't know about me thought she meant "joy" as in happiness. My family, her friends, and her family knew she was referring to me. I kept my head down during the bulk of her testimony. I really wanted to tune in to her voice; not the outfit and her mannerisms. I closed my eyes. I concentrated on her words. I can honestly say that while I listened intently, I only heard portions of what she said because my focus was in and out. My father leaned in again and said, "Man she can write!" I'm thinking, well someone will have to retell me this story because I was oblivious to much of what was said. I did record her as I knew this was history in the making.

I sat there learning about her story, her challenges, her struggles, and now I saw her strength. Here stood a woman before her church confessing her sins when she did not have to. She felt this was a responsibility that she as a leader in a Christian church owed to her congregation. That speaks volumes to the type of woman she is. That speaks volumes to her relationship with her church. That speaks volumes as a woman of God.

I came to again when she repeatedly talked about joy. By then someone had given me the box of tissues and I could see my parents becoming emotional. I listened intently and noted her use of joy and Joi. She then shared that years ago she had given a child up for adoption and blah blah blah was all I heard and then she announced that they would now be able to join her as she would now see her child for the very first time. She paid homage to my parents, acknowledged my children, and called me up. I don't know why I didn't wear flats that day. My legs were wobbly. The African drummers who were visitors for the church that day pretty much had their mouths hanging open. They had this look on their face like, "did she say what I thought she just said? Is this young woman walking up here, is this really happening?'

I walked up. We greeted one another and I almost collapsed in her arms. Then I thought she was already hobbling, I know she had a knee injury. *Joi, keep it together.* It would have been horrible if I pulled this little woman to the ground. Then my mother came over and they embraced. Then my father came over. Everyone was crying. The church service had completely stopped. A fellow adoptee who is a reporter was also present and out of the corner of my eye I see that she too had a few tissues. We took a few moments and made introductions. I met my Aunt Loretta. She is the eldest member of the family 95 years old. She is a beautiful short woman who shares my brown complexion. She smiled. I said, "you wouldn't happen to be Loretta on ancestry. com would you?" "Yes, that's me!" "I sent you a message over a year ago asking you a family-related question." She looked at me and my birth mom, she said, "I thought I knew all my family, so I just never responded." We all laughed. I began to listen to the conversations around me of those in the congregation. Two of the African drummers were adopted parents. There were a few adoptees in the audience, several people had relatives who were adopted, or had close friends who were in some way shape or form touched by adoption. Then there was our lifesaver, Ms. Richardson with EJay Photography who captured it all in pictures. I think my Aunt captured much of it on video and I made an audio recording. Church service was closed out with song and prayer.

Flo took off her African headpiece as we spoke at the altar. It reminded me of a Tyler Perry moment when one of his characters is talking and takes off her wig because she is hot. All of the crying and emotion made us all hot that February morning. *Yup, she looks just like my mom.* I told her that I was confused when we arrived at the church. I couldn't tell if that was her with the hat and the garb. I shared with her how my dad reacted when I showed him her picture. He thought she looked so much like my mom. We were in the basement one day and his eyes literally popped out of his head when he saw her Facebook picture. He leaned forward in his chair, I thought he was going to fall out. All he kept saying was, "Joi, Joi do you see this?" She said, I might have hat head at the moment but this thing is hot." I laughed hard. There was the salt and pepper hair that I was looking for when I arrived.

I think Flo also has the strange jawline that I have. I'm trying not to stare but my book about adoption reunions mentioned that I would stare and everyone else would stare at me too. I scanned every part of her face and head that is now visible. When I modeled in college and put my modeling portfolio together the photographers would occasionally take pictures with our hair slicked back and in a full men's suit. That was always a huge step for me because I did not like my forehead. Slicking my hair back only made the forehead much more obvious but the photographers and designers loved that androgynous look.

I knew modeling was a brutal business but no one prepared me for people picking apart your pictures and identifying your flaws. Their job was to identify the flaws that they had to cover up with makeup or shoot around you at a different angle so the flaw would not stand out in photographs. It was a review of my contact sheet when the photographer and the agent were going through my pictures with a magnifying glass that I learned that one side of my jaw was fuller than the other. Then I learned that when in fitted pants, one hip went straight in and the other was curved. It was during that review that the agency told me I was deemed to have great hands and nails for hand photos and that I had a great head for hats and wigs because of my forehead. As I looked at Flo, I saw one full cheek and one flat cheek. When Ms. Richardson took a picture, at first my birth mom stood to my left. In the next set of pictures she asked Ms. Richardson if she would take another set of pictures because she was so excited with the first set that she did not stand on her best side. Ms. Richardson started laughing and began to take more photos.

I wanted to ask Flo at that moment if she switched to the other side because one jaw is fuller than the other or was it something else. I have always heard people say their best side. I think I need to figure out mine. In some of my pictures, I look like a straight up guppy fish. That look always comes shining through when I take pictures especially with my Sorority sisters at our line reunions. They all look cute and I look like a blowfish. I'm physically smaller than all of them but in the pictures, I look bigger than some of them. The sad part about my photographic woes is that I modeled all through college. You would think I knew something about posing. I only have a few great pictures that show a nice jawline. Tasha always tells me it's that I don't know my angles and that I don't know how to use the light to make it work for me. Unfortunately, she is the worst at showing people how to do something, so she can never tell me or explain what I should be doing. She can only tell me if it's wrong. Her favorite line "How can you not know this? You were a professional model."

I was most uncomfortable in front of a camera unless they were candid shots. So I said to my birth mom, "It's funny that you mention your better side. I still don't know what side is my better side. My daughters have been trying to help me figure out what side works best for me." We took more pictures. Ms. Richardson captured action shots, posed shots, the congregation, the African drummers and all of the emotional chaos. My mothers are flanked on each side of me. They are the same complexion, same height, same color hair this is crazy and I'm looking down at both of them. All those years I thought I might see my birth mom in a fashion catalog... absolutely not! Flo is five feet six inches tall. Now that we are up close and personal, I see that she and I have the same nose and smile. I don't know if my mothers will be uncomfortable with the constant comparison, but God knows they really look alike. Looking like my mother was the one thing that helped as I grew up. No one would have ever guessed that she was not my mother which made the pairing look legitimate. Yet when you put me next to her nieces and nephews, The Alston's they all favor and I didn't match up with them.

A year and a half after the reunion while sitting in a group session I learned that back in the '70s that matching birth parents to the looks of the adopted parents was by design. Every day, week, month, meeting I learned something new about my adoption journey. I can't stop looking back and forth between the two of them. Now that family and friends are starting to meet Flo, that is the first thing they come over and whisper to me, it never fails. And it's always a whisper. My father's reaction by far was the best.

Voilà, Medical History!

When we went out to a local diner after church. Over dinner, I saw Flo her eat a dish with tomatoes. I can't touch a tomato. We talked about allergies. She shared that she can eat cooked tomatoes, but not a raw tomato. The last time I ate a tomato was twenty years ago in college after a basketball game when someone brought a pizza that I couldn't resist. I was starving thinking, *what's the worst that could happen?* I started eating the slice. All seemed to be going well until I got to the first bite of the second piece. I began to have my very own Will Smith allergic reaction like from the movie *Hitch. What was I thinking? Joi, you are a fool. You have not eaten pizza in years.* My roommate, Renee, came back to the parking lot. I motioned to get me to the room quick I need a dose of Benadryl. The swelling went down and I slept the rest of that night. My pizza reaction is running through my head as I sat and watched her eat that dish with the tomato sauce. I wondered if it's time for me to try tomatoes again. We spent a lot of time talking about allergies. One thing that I did learn is that I have allergies that are a combination of the ones she has and her sister's allergies.

After about five months of treatment, I realized that my allergist never gave me a full list of my allergies. My list of allergies goes on and on and I now see some of the irritants to my body are not actually food allergies, so there is a great chance that one day I can eat a real slice of pizza. During dinner, I had to tell my birth mom and my Aunt that one of the main questions all my girls want to be answered is which birth parent was responsible for their allergies. Over the years I always told them don't blame me, blame my gene pool. Never did I imagine I'd be sitting down with members of my birth family having this discussion. I later told my daughters that we get our allergies from my birth mom. Tasha said, "Oh that's who we need to blame for this". I told Tasha, "Flo also mentioned when she eats raw tomatoes that her lips swell." Tasha's eyes got big as she shook her head.

Every allergic characteristic that my birth mom or my Aunt described or story they told if it wasn't my issue it was a similar issue my girls had. In my mind, I'm checking off these similarities trying to remain attentive during this dinner conversation. My parents sat across from my birth mom and me, and my Aunt sat across from me.

In hindsight, that wasn't a good idea because then I couldn't look at her. I was so glad my parents came to dinner. At first, my Dad was like you two may want to be alone and talk. That was not my plan. My parents were there both social butterflies, they can talk, they tend to be the life of the party, they are good with keeping the energy light and fun. I needed them there.

After my birth mom and my Aunt shared their allergy stories, I shared with them that it wasn't until my youngest daughter Tasha was in second or third grade that I figured out how to tell when she had eaten something she was allergic too. It was weird there were days that Tasha talked about not feeling well or saying that her throat felt scratchy. Her father and I tried to figure out what she ate for the day. He shared with me what he had given her and I shared with him what I had given her or saw her eat. When we asked her what she ate at school there were never any concerns on our part about the food selections she was making.

We began to get concerned and I became more attentive to monitoring when her reactions occurred because the doctor said if she is swelling on the outside, who knows what it is doing to her on the inside? We set in motion a plan to monitor her food intake without telling her that's what we were doing. I had run out of checks and decided to use the online system to put money on the girls' lunch accounts. While putting money on their account that weekend I noticed at the top of the screen that there was a tab that allowed me to see their exact purchases. I scrolled through all three girls lists. I observed patterns on Tasha's lunch items: pizza every Friday and enjoying chocolate chip cookies at least every other day. I decided to wait until Friday when she came home to see what her lips would look like. BAM! I was correct. Her lips were swollen as a result of eating something she was allergic to. I took her to the doctor to discuss this allergic reaction and possible harm inside her body. He advised Tasha to monitor what she eats. He told her any outside swelling is the outward appearance of what is happening inside her body. He showed her pictures of the needles that would be used if her reactions continued. I continued monitoring what she was eating as I was also testing her ability to tell the truth.

This mysterious swelling was only happening when she went to school. Never on the weekend. Never over break. Whoala her lunch account told me the entire story as I went back into the account and looked up her purchases. She was eating chocolate chip cookies three times as much as she was eating pizza. I soon learned she was selectively honest with what she ate. The more swollen her lips were the more likely she was to say what she ate that day. It wasn't until she might have been in fourth grade that I told her that I knew exactly why her lips were swollen. I waited until she came home on Friday. Tasha's lips were very swollen off her face. By middle school and high school, Tasha and Jasmin learned how to plan when they were going to eat certain foods. They learned the power of following the food up with lots of water to flush out their system. Tasha did not want an EpiPen and I did not want to have to give it to her.

As my birth mom talked about her lips, I looked at her face and her lips were shaped like mine and the girls. I couldn't wait to tell Tasha and Jasmin about their new grandmother's allergic reactions. She also mentioned hives and that is right up Jasmin's alley. All the girls' life we have had a dog. It wasn't until Jasmin went off and went to college that we learned how allergic Jasmin was to her dog Diva. When Jasmin lived in the house I guess her body adapted to it. When she went off to college and then came home one weekend you would have thought the girl was going to die. Her eyes were nearly closed, she was sneezing, and she was beginning to break out in hives yet she refused to put "her dog" out of her room. Jasmin's reactions sounded similar to another story my birth mom told.

As she and I walked out of the restaurant she shared that my birth father had sinus issues in college and she often called him Sniffles. Between both of them, I was just doomed for all this allergy mess. I'm currently trying different allergy shots. I'm learning some of the things I react to are irritants to my body and not necessarily allergies. I'm on this plan to get one allergy shot a week for two years. They inject you with everything you are allergic to. The theory is that this will build up my immune system and the things that I'm allergic to, my body will no longer react to them or the irritants.

A year and a half after our reunion we were celebrating together in Philadelphia for Traci's graduation from Rowan University. We are at an outdoor bar off a pier. It was partly open and partially covered. Tasha picked this spot because they have music and she loved the view. I guess she didn't think much about the weather forecast because this was an outdoor facility and on this day, it rained. *Why did we listen to, eighteen year old, Tasha? Sometimes I really don't know.* She provided no details about this place except it was the perfect place. She asked me if I was getting married soon and if I was I should consider this location for an after party. She has such a convincing personality and here we all are sitting in the rain at a bar on the pier for Traci's graduation gathering.

Neither of my mother's bottoms hit the chair before some heavy set dude at least fifteen years their junior came over and asked if he could dance with one of the *twins*. He talked about them being double-trouble and gave them hugs. We fell out laughing. Now, which of the two do you think got up and danced around with him right in the middle of the bar doing the hustle? Momma Flo! She did get up and they danced a little. Like my students, I definitely videotaped that moment and sent it to Jasmin who wasn't with us. We were in tears laughing. He said he was so lucky to have seen twins, he thanked her for the dance and brought them a drink. *Did you hear me when I said their butts hadn't even hit the stool before they are getting approached at the bar.*

My dad was laughing but he was more focused on getting something to eat. He refused to eat at the college. Rowan had an amazing graduation. It was brief, exciting, and they had food and beverages for all their guests. The president of the college reiterated several times that the students' graduation was a reason to celebrate and they pulled out all the stops. They had food, music, and beverages for the older crowd. My dad didn't want to ruin his appetite for the dinner after the graduation, so he didn't want to eat anything. Once we realized we were at a bar and all they had was finger foods, I thought he was going to choke poor Tasha to death. In the end, we all said the same thing, *Why did we let Tasha plan this and nobody looked into the details. Oh well, finger foods it was.* The twins were now enjoying their drink and the appetizers. The location was a great venue for a fun day out. But the rain, coupled with the fact that we were celebrating with Traci's 83- year-old grandfather, a 74-year-old grandmother, and 67- year-old grandmother, who were all expecting to sit down and eat dinner, it was not as expected. It's during those times when life gets hectic that I turn to see who will pick up the ball and come up with a plan. Right now, Tasha is zero for one!

20

A Tall Order

The Second Reunion

January 29, 2017, was a day that the pieces of my life and my story were coming together. Flo gave me the name of my birth father. I immediately reached out to cousin Pat. To this day I remember Pat saying, "He's my first cousin! You are going to love him! Joi, he is so kind! He is such a great guy. I know he doesn't know about you, he can't." I had to convince her that I know for a fact that he knew. Once she calmed down I told her how I knew she knew. Pat said that she would give him my phone number.

While Flo and I were texting, just at the moment where we both felt she and I had said enough for a first-time interaction, my phone rang. Pat didn't think he would call for a few days because he was in shock. Turns out, he called within forty-five minutes. I grabbed a notebook. I didn't have time to get nervous. He started talking and talking, and asking questions, and talking and giving me a full family history lesson. I have at least two pages of notes from our first conversation. It was overwhelming. I think we were on the phone for over two hours. Who does that? Early on something Pat said he asked her sat in the back of my mind and I was pissed at first. That famous question birth families ask about adoptees not necessarily to adoptees, "What does she want?" When she said that I became furious, but then I sat back and said let me wait to see how she addressed him because she and I have been dealing with one another for over a year. She invited me to the family reunion in Virginia last year. Oddly enough she has a home six miles away from my adopted father's mother's childhood home. How creepy was that? Add to that there a few common family surnames from that area that stood out to us. When I told my adopted father that news he said, "wouldn't that be crazy if we were actually related?" We laughed and I said, "Now that would be a story to tell!"

As my conversation with Papa John came to a close he and I discussed the next steps. He lived in the Silver Springs, Maryland area and I'm in New Jersey. He knew he and his wife were coming to New Jersey in July. In one of our early conversations, he suggested meeting at the family reunion. My first thought was now that would be crazy and probably too overwhelming for me. Then he clarified that it would be his wife's side of the family. He assured me that his wife knew of my existence. He let me know that there could be a chance at that reunion that I meet my brother and twin step-sisters, who are two years older than me. Turns out they are a year older than me and my brother is ten years younger than me. So what does that make me? Technically, I am no longer the only child, but now am I the middle child? How do you answer those types of questions? How do you respond if it comes up in an ice breaker activity? I've done things where I group kids based on their birth order for discussions. In hindsight, I would take the advice I give my own students. If you were raised as an only child but you have extended family you have to decide your group based on what you identify with most. Therefore, I would stick with the only child group. This middle child or third child group is all too new. So glad there is less of a stigma in this day and age to extended families and blended families.

It was January and we decided on June or July, whenever his wife's family reunion would take place in Atlantic City, which would be our first time to meet. In our second or third conversation, I learned that his three sisters let him have it. They could not believe he was talking to me in January, 46 years later, and here he was telling me to let's wait until the summer. Before I knew it, we were planning a gathering in mid-March. By that time I had already had my dates to meet my birth mother, Flo. She and I planned a small gathering the second Sunday in February and then a larger family gathering on the fourth Sunday in February. My schedule was kind of packed as my dad and I were rehearsing for a Rock & Soul Review at the end of March, and I was working on my new job as Assistant Principal, so life was absolutely crazy.

As we began to plan for March I knew some of the new family would be able to come and some wouldn't, so I tried not to get my hopes up. In between all these planning conversations and thoughts, I was meeting and talking to my cousin and my new Aunts. Aunt Eileen was very energetic and welcoming. She was the first to say "I've always known about you and I knew one day you would find us." There was no hesitation. No second guessing it would happen. She remembered the month I was born because it was a month before her daughter was born. She said she could never forget that. She went on to talk about the family, my new relatives and trying to set her schedule to see if she could come to New Jersey. She was the one who told me when her brother told her we would wait until July to meet at his wife's family reunion that all the sisters let him have it. She was funny and the conversation flowed easily.

Weeks later, I spoke to Aunt Lois. She too was very easy to talk to. She declared herself as the one who keeps in touch with everyone but also the one who doesn't keep in contact as much as she should. She described herself as a loner at times. Boy, do I know about that. Sometimes I feel like I could just fall into a rabbit hole and disappear. She was excited about the next steps in our trying to coordinate meeting one another. As a dentist, she didn't know what her schedule would allow, but she knew one way or another we would meet soon.

Both of my aunts had a bit of raspiness in their voices. I was tickled by that. I will never forget when I was working customer service in college. I finally met the supervisor from another department who assisted me on some of my troublesome customer calls. She and I had only spoken on the phone. One day a supervisor from a different shift came over to my cubicle to meet a few of the new folks, myself included. When she came to shake my hand she said, " Oh I'm so glad you don't look like your voice at all." My eyebrows lifted. REALLY. Now I knew my voice was a bit raspy, but REALLY. She caught me completely off guard. She said it in such a matter of fact way. All I could do was think, *shots fired, yo this lady is crazy. Straight insult straight face and all. WOW. Glad we are at work. Glad I can hold my tongue. I knew my voice was raspy lady! I was never good at whispering it just doesn't work. I was never good at disguising my voice, I could never maintain the cute soft, phone voice just didn't work for me.* My best friend Alexia, on the other hand, she could whisper and she's always had that perfect operator voice. Me talking to a guy on the phone surely never sounded "cute". I grappled with that for years. Once I realized in college that I could really sing, then I never really worried about how my speaking voice sounded. So as I heard each of my aunts speak, the light bulb went off. Here is something I struggled with internally, but never talked about, but now I can say that this raspy rough voice is in my genes! For years it was a silent struggle. Problem resolved. It's normal for me.

My conversation with my Aunts were enlightening. I learned a lot about everyone and everything in the family except for my brother. My birth father took me back to slavery. He made sure that I knew that a great, great relative was one of the Tuskegee Airmen, Spann Watson and that another relative was one of the pilots who trained the Tuskegee Airmen. He let me know that college and education have been the backbone of our family's success. Our relatives were in college in the early 1900s. My great great grandfather's degree is signed by Booker T. Washington. My Aunts and cousins were at the top of their fields; pediatrician, dentist, lawyers, HR specialist, esthetician, and education. My first cousins are doing big things, we have many entrepreneurs in the family. I felt like he was saying I need you to know that you don't come from no junk!

In everything they all said, they reiterated education. They knew I had my master's degree and to them, it was like, OK so what's next? Many family members have three degrees. During the entire conversation, I could hear my mom saying, "see, I told you so." She always told me that I was meant to do more. She always stressed that there was something about the way that I learned and dealt with things that there was more to me than the average person. Academically, at times it appeared even though I was doing well, I was afraid to go further. I'm thinking, *mom is going to love hearing about this*. I really can't believe that she's been telling me this stuff all my life. Now I see everything she's told me over the years are attributes that are naturally in this gene pool. I'm having flashbacks on all the conversations of her asking me why I don't "Just Do It" whatever *it* was.

As I hear a lot about family history, I'm still waiting to hear more about my brother. I had already gone through FB and googled him. A brother, a younger brother WOW but not much was mentioned about him or the twins, it was more about the older relatives. After a two-hour phone call, I was worn out. With each conversation, I learned more and more. He was so eager. His wife and sisters eventually told me, just so you know, he will talk your ear off. LOL.

As I was thinking so much about my reunion with my birth mom, I never anticipated a reunion with my birth father. I'm finding a lot of nonsense flowing through my mind on a daily basis. Movies and television plots usually tell adoptees that the birth father just came and left, a deadbeat dad and that the birth mom may have been one of many. Real life and real adoptee stories have taught me that our media and presentations about adoptees need an overhaul of perspective. It's such a misrepresentation of real stories. I wondered how many movies and television shows about adoption actually thought to toss around their ideas with someone who was adopted or do they just stick with the stereotypical negativity or one-sidedness. I've learned no one's story is the same.

As I thought about an adoption reunion with my birth father, despite the crazy thoughts that filled my mind, I was glad to have cousin Pat in my ear "he's a great guy", "he's kind", "he's caring", "he is loving", "you are just going to love LOVE HIM". As she spoke, I just imagined this little mouse who saw food on opposite sides of the room and she was running back and forth with information. I could feel her excitement through the phone, but back in that moment when we identified who he was, I could not handle it.

I finally found the words to say, *if you can pick it up from here with him, I can internalize the fact that I just found my birth mother.* Adding in the thoughts of a birth father, I immediately felt like I was going to stop breathing and pass out. Here I am with all these new discoveries sitting in my bedroom. This can't really be happening. The woman I've been talking to for over a year is my birth father's first cousin. She invited me to their family reunion after talking to me for a few weeks. Imagine if I would have walked in the door or into that yard and he was there. My aunts were there. The resemblance is undeniable. Imagine what that would have been like. That would have been a family reunion to remember. WOW!! Every time I think of my reunion with him, this scenario pops through my mind. I can't make this stuff up. It is only through God's divine plan that this is happening.

As we planned for my birth father and his family to come up in March I kept thinking how are my parents going to feel? Now I asked my dad if we could have this reunion at his home and he was fine with that. I was now feeling like if I'm asking my birth dad to come here, I need him to talk to my Dad first. My Dad needs to know my birth dad isn't crazy, he isn't a con artist, he isn't out there in the streets. He needs to know he is a good dude. I had been talking to my birth father weekly and got a good feel for his personality and core values, but my Dad was concerned with who was coming to his house, and what his intentions were. Whew! So I mentioned the possibility of them having a discussion with one another to both of them. I asked John since I was inviting him into my Dad's home if he would mind talking to my Dad beforehand. He acknowledged that he could understand what a father's concerns would be and he'd be glad to talk with my Dad. He always had such a positive energy. Conversations with my birth father gave me the feeling that if he were a light bulb, he would light up in excitement. He just seemed happy to be found and ready to get to know one another.

These conversations were also challenging because it was uncomfortable to refer to my parents as my parents when I was talking to my birth parents. Just weird. James and Jerlene are my parents. Then

I wonder how do my birth parents feel that I call them by their first names? Is that disrespectful? Do they get it? I always got the sense that both of my birth parents knew and respected and appreciated the great family that raised me. They refer to them as my mom and dad which was weird at first but the reality of it was that is who they are. No matter how clear people are in their titles and I'm comfortable with where we are in this stage of the game, those thoughts don't go away. I remind myself if I were married and had a relationship with my spouse's parents I'd have in-laws. Most people refer to their in-laws as mom or dad, although that was something I never did when I was married for twenty years. It is something I had hoped to one day be comfortable saying to them, but that never happened.

In my group meetings, I'm learning that these titles are fine lines all adoptees face and that adopted parents and birth parents all have their own view on this topic. I've learned that for birth parents, the mere fact of being introduced as a parent and if you have siblings for them to hear you mention their other children as your siblings is as special a moment to them. Similar to an adoptee hearing their new family refer to them as a relative. It's a validation of our existence in your life.

As we map out the plans for the reunion, I asked Jasmin, our party planner to come up with some getting to know you activities. We love to play games. Having worked in education she and I have been a part of countless professional development icebreakers so I knew Jasmin was my girl to get it done.

The day comes and the time is clicking closer to their arrival. Since I had my break down the morning of meeting my birth mother, I made sure to read a lot more of *The Adoption Reunions* book Pam recommended before meeting my birth father. At this point, I just wanted to get it done.

The doorbell rang. I was up in the bedroom with Traci. I froze. Traci looked at me. Are you going to answer it? Nope! Not ready. "Are you OK?" she asked. "Nope. Not ready!" I told Traci that it should be her Aunt Pat at the door as Papa John just called and gave me his ETA.

I asked Traci to go and entertain them for a few moments while I get myself together. Pat is very easy to talk to it should be her and her husband. "Oh wait, Traci, Pat isn't an Aunt. She is our cousin!" "Mom, I got this, you just get yourself together, take a moment. Breathe Mommy. I got you covered until you are ready to come down."

I could hear them conversing. Traci was keeping the conversation going just as much as they were. I heard lots of laughter. Pat had the same energy in her voice as she did on the phone. Eventually, I got myself together looking at the time as it was getting closer and closer to John's ETA. The build-up was intense. I came downstairs. As soon as I saw Cousin Pat, I was like this complexion thing is real. I will never forget the picture she sent me of my grandmother and all of my great aunts, "High Yellow" as people would say. She was a bit shorter than me. We talked and laughed. I had a spread of food for the event prepared and went in to check on the food. I thought I saw a car slowly passing the house. I looked at the time. This would be about right. That's them. I stayed in the kitchen knowing the doorbell would be ringing soon. By this time the girls and my parents were all at the house.

The doorbell rang. I heard his voice. He was excited to lay eyes on his granddaughter. "Well, you must be my granddaughter!" I could hear one of the girls offering to take their coats. I knew he would be approaching the intersection soon. OK do I wait? Do I go in? How does this work? I start walking toward that intersection. The family is standing in the family room and some are near the door. In an instant, we are in front of each other. My head was somewhat down. The first things I see is his hands and his long arms. We are now face to face. I looked straight ahead thinking he's my height and realize that I have to look up. As a tall person, looking up is weird for me. As my head looks up, my mom says, "Well now you know where your height comes from!" Everyone laughed. I noticed his forehead. It was like I was doomed with this big forehead. He and my birth mom have similar foreheads. Again, all those years of comments about my head. Now I know its genetic. I blame them. His skinny wrist, long fingers, complexion, I got it all honestly.

I tried hard not to stare. His wife made reference to my height and the girls' heights. At that point, I introduced him to everyone. Throughout the day a few family and friends came by. I invited our regulars and folks who can talk. I didn't want to be in this close setting for things to get quiet and awkward at any point. I knew there would be a lot of glances. I read about that in my book. I was looking at his mannerisms. It was kind of sickening to see that his body moved just like mine. Then I thought about my girls and how they move like me.

My granddaughter became the focus of attention and he began to mix up the stories I've told him about the girls to my granddaughter. It never fails that people mix them up, so I let him know there was nothing to be apologetic about when it came to calling one of them by the wrong name or by getting their scenarios mixed up.

Midway through the gathering, I asked Jasmin to bring everyone together to introduce her activity. I wanted something so that we could learn the similarities and differences of one another. Jasmin passed out her sheets, broke down the instructions and the games began. As friends and family arrived we handed them their pencil and paper and the activity continued. All three generations of the family were actively engaged. No one was allowed to sit this one out. After time was called Jasmin and I called the group back to attention and we began to identify people in the room who met the characteristics on our sheet and they began to share the conversation they had with the other person. Knowing everyone in the room and having been given some insight into my new family I sat back and watched as I knew they had similarities with many of the folks in the room. At one point I went upstairs and watched from the balcony as the room was full of energy.

We thanked everyone for their participation and then John asked if he could make a presentation. As we gathered, he pulled out several picture frames. He presented me with framed pictures of my grandparents and a framed copy of my great great grandfather's college diploma, with three copies inside the back of the frame for each of the girls when their homes were established. He also presented us with several books that included the historical references of a few great

great uncles as well. We were blown away. It was a powerful message. John is a talker and at some point, his wife said, "Now OK John," so he began to wrap up. We began to talk about one of the things we learned about my cousin and her husband which was how they met at a hand dancing lesson. Without prompting, we put on the music and they began to share their stuff. Next thing I know my mom and aunts were jumping in taking his hand as they danced around the room. By that point, John asked about our upcoming show so we put on the music and my father began to sing his legendary version of "You Will Never Find Another Love Like Mine" by Lou Rawls. The girls became his back-up dancers. We had a wonderful time.

The crowd began to leave and the evening ended with all of us just sitting around laughing and talking. It was a day to remember. We talked about the upcoming show again and they said they were coming. So it was confirmed. In two weeks I'd have my newfound blended family together again at this event.

The magnitude of having everyone together for the show didn't dawn on me until it hit me that I didn't know my adoption story or how their relationship ended. So this could be a good or bad thing from either of their perspectives. Now, this issue became another thing for me to figure out. How do I tell each of them that the other person is going to be there? How do I keep them away from one another? How will this go down? All eyes will be on Flo and John's reaction. Thankfully, the light bulb came on and assured me that I don't have to worry about that. It was 46 years ago! That's not my issue. That's their issue. I have to let grown folks be grown folks and as a courtesy give them the heads up, but will not worry about their issues or things I cannot control. Besides, I have to think about my performance. This will definitely be a performance of a lifetime.

My emotions were still in overdrive. I was trying not to think about the fact that I was singing and had not sung in a while. *What was I thinking? It's on the big stage! How am I going to capture this moment*? I soon learned that my Aunt Lois was also coming. I was looking forward to putting a face to the voice. I had seen a few pictures from the fish fry they had in the summer and we definitely resembled each other. I couldn't wait and I was not going to worry. I had to convince myself that if anything negative happens it is not my fault. *Okay. STOP Joi! You're talking and talking and haven't asked God to help you at all. Practice what you preach. If you're going to pray, then don't worry. If you're going to worry, then don't pray.* That night with all of these thoughts going on inside my head, I knew this was so much bigger than me. I needed to have a serious talk with God.

Lord, help me find the words to share with all my parents that the other will be present at this show. Help me find words of comfort as I don't know my adoption story. In my birth parents' silence I could worry but, thus far, I've seen that they both are of good sound mind and heart, so I'm trusting that you will take care of this. Allow me to pray this prayer and leave it with you. Let the words of my mouth and the meditations of my heart be pleasing and acceptable in thy sight. I don't know what I was thinking when I invited all of them. But God, I know you've got my back. To be able to even have this conversation in prayer is a miracle in itself. I'm learning that when I am obedient and leave it with you, that you handle it. I realized that I hadn't been praying about this and today I stop and leave it in prayer practicing what I preach. I thank you for what you have already done and for what you are about to do in my life. In Jesus name, I pray. AMEN AMEN AMEN!

I knew that although I prayed and was leaving it before God, that did not mean I didn't need to act; faith without work is dead. Knowing I didn't have a lot of time after meeting John, I decided to talk with each of my parents about my new found realization that all of them will be in one place in a few weeks. I spoke with my mom first and her answer is always, "It is what it is. It will work out don't worry about it." My dad was like, "Yeah I wondered if you realized they would both be there together. Hey, I'll be with you behind the stage so I guess we will hear about how it goes." Then I told my birth parents. I reiterated that the place was a county theater and they may not come in contact with one another, but that at the end of the show when everyone is waiting for the cast, that's when they may see one another so I asked them to mentally prepare.

It was at that time my birth father shared that he and Flo had communicated after my birth. I asked how he thought my stepmom would do and he expressed no concerns. I shared with my birth mother the same information and we talked. She knew her sister would be there in case she needed to step away and became overwhelmed. You never know what is going to surface in these situations. I assured her that the place was big but after the show, there would be no getting around them seeing one another so also told her to mentally prepare. I reiterated to both of them that due to the nature of these circumstances those who know of the situation may be watching to see their interactions with one another. I then take my mind back to the fact that I will be behind the stage, so I won't see this go down. I wondered if there was any beef with his current wife or did she come along long after? Hmmm I don't know. Right now I don't want to know. I am going to leave that alone.

As the show approached, my father asked me how I felt about ALL my family coming together. I told him that they are all grown and responsible for their own actions and that I have enough to worry about with singing these songs, so I wouldn't worry about it. I did tell him that I let each of them know the other would be there, so they would have time to process their thoughts for themselves because I didn't know their history. Then I laughed and said, "But those who know will be watching like a hawk. I'm sure they will see each other but they shouldn't or probably won't need to interact with one another until after the show when folks wait around." He and I reiterated that the place was big so there shouldn't be a problem.

It's showtime! Before the doors opened, management informed us that they didn't have as many sales as they anticipated and ticket purchasers from different levels would be moved to the main level. I immediately thought about Flo and John but with the show about to begin, I went back to rehearsing my song. During the opening number, I didn't want to look for folks in the crowd but I could see it was an intimate crowd and people were spread across the front three sections. I couldn't make out any faces because the lights were bright and the music was loud. *Enjoy the moment Joi.*

The show was great! My father, as usual, was a fan favorite. This 80+-year-old dude crooning with ladies dancing behind him, and oh Lord, I had to follow him. The ladies and I had been having issues with our harmonies and the pitchiness. After the rehearsal earlier in the day, the music director told me that our song was his deceased brother's favorite song. I reminded him a few weeks before that the song I first sang with them was "Heatwave"by Martha and the Vandellas, which I wanted to sing, but he insisted on me singing "This Will Be," by Natalie Cole. So I did the best I could with it and decided even if we get to high and crash and burn, that I should just have fun. Then I thought about all my parents watching. My mom's words came to me, *it is what it is.* I was having issues singing the song, but on to the next segment of the show.

In the finale, we sing "Love Train" and run through the aisles. Yes, I was running in heels and a dress around the theater. I laughed because we hadn't performed this show in over ten years and here we were ten years older running through the aisles. My dad and one of the older ladies stayed on stage at the mics. It really was a great show. The crowd had a ball. As I ran through the crowd I spotted a few faces. You invite people but never know who is going to show up but as I ran through and then stood up front I could see my people spread all over the theater. This was by far a historical moment in my life. The New Jersey legislation changed in January, I heard from each of my birth parents on January 29th, Here we were in March with ALL of my parents, my children, and a host of relatives and friends in this one room watching my father and me perform. In the end, it all worked out. My birth parents were cordial and dealt with their meeting in their own way. At some point, they will have to stop and talk to one another. I don't know what that looks or how it will work but it only seems logical.

Lord thank you for allowing me to persevere and stay true to my word of not worrying. This level of stress could have taken me way off balance. I can't explain or find the words other than "interesting" to express what my heart feels through this journey. This is unreal. All of this carries with it a boatload of communication and a lot of responsibility. The one thing that I've heard from each of them is that they are following my cues. After hearing another adoptee talk about feeling like they were living a double life, I told all my parents that I'm not living like that. All of us are going to figure out how to make this work. I needed everyone to play nice in the sandbox but also acknowledge the impact that these reunions and our coming together may dredge up within themselves. I reiterated the importance of them reading *The Adoption Reunion Handbook*. I told them that the great thing about the book is that it is broken up into sections specifically for all three members of the adoption consolation. Therefore, if they read a section on the other two components of the adoption consolation, that will give them insight into what the others are going through. I certainly don't have all the answers to this mess but I sure did my research and was attentive in groups as I listened to adopted parents and birth parents talk. I had to realize that while I was at the center of all this newness, I wasn't the only one with deep feelings behind it all. This is definitely storybook stuff that I know beyond a shadow of a doubt is nothing but God!

21

A Window of Opportunity

Crisis and Support Group Meeting January 12, 2019

I checked out Dictionary.com to see the actual definition of crisis. So often we use the word crisis very loosely. I wanted to make sure the labeling of my circumstances was accurate. This site defined crisis as "a stage in a sequence of events at which the trend of all future events, especially for better or for worse, is determined." It went on to say that it is the "turning point or a dramatic emotional or circumstantial upheaval in a person's life." Looking back, my adoption journey has had me operating in crisis mode for quite some time.

During what would have been the two-year anniversary of my silent celebration of the date I received my original birth certificate, my oldest daughter Jasmin, was in the middle of a crisis in her life. She called on my birth mom Flo to make a visit for the weekend to help. Normally, we don't call on my birth mom without notice as everything with her so planned out, because chances are she's not going to be available. So while we have recently become spur of the moment folks, we now see why we are all so calendared crazy; this mess must be genetic.

My schedule was full that day so when Jasmin mentioned that Nana was coming up for the weekend to stay with us, I was flustered. I had a sorority meeting and an adoption group meeting, which meant that I would be out all day. I didn't say it to her, but I was thinking, *Lord, why? Of all weekends you bring her up it's a weekend that I have a packed day?* Then it hit me. I could ask Flo to come to my adoption support group meeting.

Then I thought, *no, not a good idea.* She was very clear when I asked her about counseling, talking about my adoption story, or speaking about how all of this came to be. At that time, she said she was not ready and not interested. Yet that small voice inside me told me to forget about what she said in the past. I wanted to be a little selfish. My mom always told me to stop worrying about other people's feelings and what they thought of my decisions. If she says no, what's the worst that could happen? I believe I would get over it. After all, this is our 2nd anniversary weekend. I wonder if she even recognized that. Oh well, there is no way that she could know the significance of this weekend because she doesn't know when I got my original birth certificate.

If anything, I hope she knows the date that's coming up, January 29th. This is the date that she and I first spoke and the date she gave me the name of my birth father. So for the next 20 minutes, I sat at the kitchen counter going back and forth in my mind as to whether or not to ask her to attend. She's a talker, and the adoption group is really a great bunch of people, so if she comes, she will definitely enjoy it. I bet without even realizing it, once she starts talking, she is going to be running her mouth more than she imagined.

There's just something dynamic about being in a room with other adoptees, birth parents, and adopted parents. I made up my mind. I told Jasmin that was going to ask Flo to attend. Jasmin thought it was a good idea. I had to kick off the year at a sorority meeting with my Sorors, then from there, I would leave early and go to the support group meeting. Jasmin's house is near my sorority chapter meeting, so this would work out great.

I messaged Flo via instant message and text message. It was getting late, but I that saw she was logged into the app. I was going to put in a whole bunch of explanations as to why she should come. Then I thought I wanted to keep it simple so that her only response would be yes or no. There is nothing more to it than that. Would you like to go to the adoption support group today with me, yes or no?

I was feeling apprehensive and doubling back on my decision to ask her. I was talking to Jasmin and I was just about to tell her that she might want to plan something to do with Flo in the event she doesn't want to attend the group meeting. Before I could finish getting the words out, her response came through that read "SURE" in all caps! I was startled. I literally had to look back at what I asked her. Does this really mean she is going to come to the meeting? She must be half asleep and didn't fully read my message. Does this really say "SURE"? I had butterflies in my stomach. *Don't question it Joi, take it and run with it. Don't make a big deal out of it or she will rethink this thing.* So I sent back what I had to do prior to the meeting for my sorority and told her that I'd swing by and pick her up afterward.

It was exciting being back in the new year seeing our meeting filled with women in their business attire. There is something special about the Central Jersey Alumnae chapter. You can be away for a while and always come back to a warm welcome. Between working Saturday events and attending the adoption support group, something always runs up against this meeting date. I made a decision in 2019 to mesh the two. I would attend part of the chapter meeting and part of the adoption group meeting each month.

For the past two years, I thought I was going full fledge sorority meetings on Saturday's because I still needed that reconnection to people. Yet I realized that my mental health was a priority and I needed my mind and heart right sooner than later. So, if I was going to eventually work on being a good sorority sister and a willing worker, I had to get "me" right first. This was out of character for me. Normally, I would have forsaken myself and stayed busy with work and active in my organizations. I kept up a hectic schedule during the heat of the craziness in my life. I stayed busy 24/7, to avoid going home. I knew then that it wasn't good for me, and I was also sure that if I went back into a work overload lifestyle, I'd be falling into the same trap that led to my burn out.

I shared with a few sorors that they may see me now and then on a Saturday, but not often. Once I started going to the support group, I never missed a meeting for one year. It always felt like each month there was something going on and I couldn't miss a session. At times, there were things I needed to express, and at other times there were things I just needed to hear. I often came in with questions as I was always trying to analyze my feelings.

Then I got to the point where I felt I could jump into a few sorority meetings and see what happens if I miss a support group session. After all, I now had two support groups and personal counseling. I found a way to get involved consistently with our arts and letters committee. "Consistently" is the key word because I don't like to do anything half-baked. For years, if I couldn't do things consistently, I had no problem saying no.

The funny thing about it is that every time I thought about leading a group, God kept telling me to work on myself. Being a mom has always caused me to focus on taking care of others. Even when God was whispering in my ear for me to focus on me, I didn't listen. Whenever I pushed God's instruction aside, something would happen that let me know I should have never been involved in XYZ in the first place. I've learned to listen to my intuition, that gut feeling, and things seem to work out much better for me. Although my gut doesn't always make sense, the outcomes are far better than what I had planned to do. I'm happy to say that I am finally learning how to get out of my own way.

The entire sorority meeting I was checking the clock, waiting for 12:30 to hit so I could step out. I tried to stay focused in the meetings, but all I could think about was that Flo said, "SURE" in response to my request. *Does she realize what she is getting into? Do I need to call her and tell her how this group works? That people actually talk. She does realize she's going to be in a room where people are talking about adoption. She hasn't even told me my adoption story. Is she really going to attend or just back out at the last minute*? Were constant nagging thoughts.

The clock struck 12:30! Wouldn't you know that they would be talking about a topic I wanted to hear about? I waited a few more minutes until the end. Then I tiptoed past a few people, exchanged a few hugs and kept it moving. Man, I wish I could stay for the committee reports. Hundreds of women in a meeting reviewing programs, social action items, health and wellness programs, technology programs for seniors, youth events, and upcoming community service events for the counties that we serve. It doesn't get any better than this. I finally exit the building and speed walk to the car. It is freezing and I had to park on the street. The meeting was at Washington Community School, which has a small parking lot so we often spill over into the street parking. I love having a remote start to warm up the car from a distance. This was by far the best extra expense on a car ever. I highly recommend it.

I texted her to let her know that I was en route, but that we were going to be late. I emailed Tom, Pam, and Tina once she said she was coming. Tina wrote the article in the NJ Monthly about my experience a few years ago and she came to the church when we first met. Tom has been a great support to me by sharing his story and offering advice and feedback as I go through my journey. Pam is the Queen Mother from NJCARE. Pam and her team are the reason that all of this happened. While she doesn't always attend the meetings, I did not want Pam to hear about it later that my birth mom was at the meeting. If anything, I thought not informing her in advance would be disrespectful. I have great respect for Pam and the legislative team with NJ CARE because my journey would not have been possible without their dedicated efforts.

Pam and I exchanged texts and she asked if she could take pictures because the group is a private group. I was fine with photos because I've told my birth mom in the past that there are things about our journey that are going to be in my book, as this adoption reunion has changed the trajectory of my life. Flo said, "as long as it is for you and your work I'm open to that." I didn't mention the picture taking part in the car as I imagined Flo might really panic and change her mind.

I pulled up at Jasmin's and honked the horn. I knew it would take a few minutes for Flo to get to the car because she walks with a cane. Walking with a cane was the one thing that made my girls think she was old, but the cane is the result of a knee injury. She is actually younger than my mother and father. I'm really bothered that after several unsuccessful surgeries, she is missing out on the things that she loved to do, like dancing, swimming and always on the go.

Once Flo gets settled into the car, we talk about everything except where we are going. I can't risk her saying, "pullover I changed my mind." It's a 35-minute drive, so I know we have more than enough time to catch up on things. We pull in behind the library. I forgot that they have a gravel parking lot. *How is this going to work with this cane? It's a good thing there are small pebbles.* She took her time as we approached the Morristown Library entrance. We walked in laughing and I realized that we needed to settle down. She was chatting with a lady simultaneously walking in. We made our way to the elevator and headed to the second floor. As we exited the elevator, there were footprints on the ground, but I didn't see the usual room. Then there was a sign on the door, Adoption Support Group. The meeting had already started and I heard someone say, "Number nine is talking." I signed both of us in and I hand Flo the sheet of rules. Queen Mother Pam is right at the door with camera in hand.

Once I got settled, I looked at my number and it was thirteen. If that person speaking was number nine, then there was a chance that no one picked ten or eleven and we would be required to speak sooner than I anticipated. I wanted Flo to get comfortable and listen for a while. I sat with number thirteen in my hand. Then, number ten was talking. At that moment, I couldn't risk us going next, so I grabbed the box with bottle caps and began shaking it so I could swap my number. I pulled it out and there were two numbers stuck together. I did not look at the number yet, but figured that out of the two, one of them had to be higher than thirteen. They called out the next number and Flo leaned in and said, "what number do you have?" I didn't know. I hadn't looked at it yet. I could see Pam looking at me as well. I showed Flo my two numbers stuck together. One was blank and the other was twenty-eight. Whew! This number gave us some time to get settled and for Flo to listen.

As others were talking, I could hear Flo let out a "Hummmm, Well, or Oh my." She even mumbled a few times, "it couldn't be me," when folks shared some really rude things said to them. When I readjusted myself in my seat I could see we moved alike. When we laughed, I didn't hear it, but we both were cracking up at something and she said, "you know we laugh alike." That one hadn't caught my attention as an observation until she said it. It's weird when my grown daughters and I say things alike, move alike, or when my mother and I say things at the same time with the same tones in our voice. Now to have my birth mom here pointing out our similarities, it's extra weird.

At that moment, I remembered the Sunday my two younger daughters met Flo. They were away at school and didn't get a chance to meet her the first time around. Yet the second time around, Flo's nieces said something to us about a sneeze she heard during the church service. Traci let out this loud noise earlier. After service, my cousin asked if it was me and I fell out laughing because she said to her sister, "one of them sneezes like Flo." Genes are a crazy thing!

More people were talking around the circle and I could see Flo was just taking it all in. I got a sense of what resonated with her based on her comments and laughter. She leaned in and asked if my parents had ever come to one of the sessions. I gave her a weird look and said, "no." I think the challenge for most people in coming to this kind of group is that it leads to extended conversations regarding the search and re-union process and the emotional impact it has had on you. This group is real talk about the things that may or may not bother you. Therefore, participation requires folks to admit and say what they are feeling and to be in the headspace to hear the things others may say about the behaviors of adopted parents, birth parents, adoptees, half-siblings, extended family, and others. I believe part of being ready for this group or any support group, means that you have to be open to saying something about this experience that makes you uncomfortable and you want to talk about it in an open forum and get honest feedback from others. The great thing about group meetings is that there are all representations of the adoption triad, so you are never alone.

It's my turn. I begin to double-back on my journey for those who had never been in our group meeting. I then share that the holidays presented some challenges for me as I was at a whole new level of trying to make time for family because my family doubled in a two year period. I shared my own struggles with developing relationships over time. While it seems like two years was a long time ago, we are actually at the beginning of our journey. I'm always reminded that folks who have been in reunion ten and fifteen years are still learning to manage time and relationships as they are getting to know strangers who we are genetically connected to them.

While I can't go into other people's stories from the group, it is always a blessing to hear others speak. I also repeatedly hear stories of folks saying that during reunion, oftentimes the adoptees and the birth parents have a hard time finding that one-on-one time, as so many folks want to get to know the new people in their lives and the adoptee often feels challenged on how to get this done without hurting anyone's feelings or spending too much time with one family over the other. I know that is something that I have to work on, but that is something I had to work on with my parents to begin with.

Since I talk all day at work, when I come home I need to decompress and just have time to myself. I don't want to have to think. I don't want to debate. I don't want to have to do anything but have complete downtime. My girls grew up knowing that about me. I made sure at 7:00 PM I enjoyed my hour of *Oprah* and that was before all of the adoption stuff. So, no I have not been very interested in talking about these different gatherings after they happen. My mind still can't wrap itself around the fact that I just had lunch with my birth mother and ate dinner with members of the legislative team that helped get the law passed. Or I just left my birth father's house as we passed through his area on a road trip. Or my Dad just asked how my birth father was and what I was doing with my birth mom for the holidays.

It's still like, *is this all really happening*? Unfortunately, the best way for me to deal with it is to just keep going with the flow. It's almost like I don't want to reflect on some of this, but thank God for a great counselor who can help me sort this mess going on in my mind and heart because, at times, I still feel like I'm going crazy. Anyway, after I spoke

I asked Flo if she wanted to speak. I introduced her and just let her go. All I could think of was that this wasn't supposed to even happen. She came to visit by chance to help my oldest daughter and here she is sharing pieces of my adoption story that I had never heard. I felt like a thermometer. The red part inside was slowly rising as my emotional rollercoaster was doing flips, but I had to maintain my composure so that I could hear and take in what she said.

I looked down most of the time and just listened, adjusting myself several times in my seat. In true form, comments and questions were taken afterward. She got hit with some doozies from other birth moms. Not that they were bad questions, but they surely were the type of questions that if you never spoke about your situation before, you would be uncomfortable answering them in a public forum. To my surprise, they asked and she answered. I heard a big gulp followed by a WOW with one of the questions, but she answered it again revealing part of my adoption story that I wasn't aware of.

After we spoke, our facilitator Tom recognized Pam for leading the grassroots efforts to make a couple of the reunions in the room possible. Pam's selfless acts as an advocate and 34 years of her dedication are priceless. I know the toll that acts of service can take on your family, your relationships, as you fight for the rights of others. I think it's important for those of us who are benefiting from her work and the work of the legislative teams to share with them how they've personally been helped.

It was important for me to contact Pam and Tom before the meeting to let them know that my birth mom was coming. Especially for Pam to know that we would be there because I wanted her to see that her work has and will impact hundreds of thousands of lives since I know that I'm going to be talking about her for a lifetime and hope to share with others all that I'm learning about adoption sensitivity. I also wanted her to know our family lifts her in prayer. It's almost like the pro athlete who retires. The bright lights are gone, the crowds dwindle down, your body is tired, you've aged, the calls decrease, the activity of your day lessens, you've given your best to your work, and then you find that you are now rebuilding your new life. It is my hope that in some small way Pam knows that her work and efforts have a lasting impact beyond what she could ever imagine.

After the meeting, we both were again greeted by various members as we always do to one another. My birth mom Flo got to have a little private conversation with folks I had been talking to for two years. Then we agreed to join them for lunch which I hadn't done in the past but thought it would be a good time to decompress. The meetings are emotionally draining.

Lunch conversation was great. Lots of warmth and laughter. On our way to dinner, Pam joined us for the ride and my birth mom shared her true feelings once she said yes to coming and then shared her fears as we prepared to exit the car and enter the library headed to the meeting. We laughed as I shared with her that I was not going to stop and ask her anything about her certainty of attending the meeting on our way, nor once we got there because I didn't want to give her a chance to back out. We all laughed again. Pam shared that she got some great pictures. I told them both that I would have to write about this once I'm able to soak it all in. This was not supposed to happen. But God.

LESSON FIVE

THE JOY OF LOVE

God's Love

If you take a look at where you were
You'll wonder how you made it through
There's no other reason for it,

It's Gods love that pulled you through
It's Gods love that carried you
It's Gods love that helped you

I can't say I didn't have my doubts
For many years I struggled with the truth
How could one believe in what you do
and never have seen you?

To some, it may sound strange
But I've come to love him and praise his name
With God in your life
He'll help you deal with all stress and strife

If he can do it for me
He can do it for you
You can't deny him, you've got to try him
God will be good to you
My God will be good to you

it's Gods love that pulled you through
it's Gods love that carried you or God's love will carry you
it's Gods love that helped you...

- Joi R. Fisher

22

Full Circle

Looking back, I can't explain the sense of peace that came over my spirit when I received my original birth certificate. After realizing that I actually had a first and last name, for the first time in my life, I felt I was finally complete. At that moment, it didn't matter to me if Flo did not want to see me. It didn't matter to me if I learned the truth about why my birth mother created an adoption plan for me. All I knew was that there was a person, another human being, who based on my birth certificate, knew that she was pregnant during her first month of pregnancy. She also had prenatal care during her first month. After all these years I was not worthless! I meant something to her. She took care of herself while she carried me.

I also saw that she listed my birth father as unknown. Why did she put that information on the adoption agency records but not on my birth certificate? Was he really who she thought my father was? The agency papers said they were sort of together until she gave birth. So did he just up and leave her? While the birth certificate made me feel legitimate, it also raised a lot of questions. I try not to dwell on my birth parents past relationship. Yet it is crazy how Flo's personal truth is a key part of my life story and her telling me so that I can share my journey obviously puts her out there too. I know there are intricate details. I know there are things that she didn't tell my birth father. I know the joys and pains of carrying a child. I know that your body after birth doesn't let you forget that you just had a baby. I also know the emotions after birth don't let you forget you had a baby. I've learned through various research that the trauma caused at separation at birth has a lasting effect on the psyche of a newborn baby.

As I sat in the stillness of my bedroom just thinking about what having this name means after years of looking day in and day out at people in the world scanning for similarities to those around me. I felt a special kind of love in my heart and thoughts of appreciation and limitless talent flowed through my mind. *I'm good at what I do now. Can you imagine the beast I'm going to be once I know who I really am? Can you imagine once I find out my quirks are not quirks but things that run in my family, how in place these once out of place characteristics made me feel? Can you imagine once I begin to believe in myself that my life was worth something to her that I will begin to feel that I deserve more from others than I allowed myself to believe I deserved?* I don't know if that makes sense to someone from the outside looking in, but for the life of me, and this sounds weird but as cute as I heard others say I was, I never believed it.

I am looking forward to my new life feeling whole. I look forward to improving my relationships, my friendships, and my connections to people. The more relatives I have met as time has passed helped me to feel free. I was no longer hiding. I could say, "I'm adopted" and not be ashamed. I could say, "Yes, I love to sing because I know singing is in my blood. Yes, I love to dance and the love of the arts runs in my family. Yes, I love school and learning, hey my birth father's great great grandfathers college diploma is signed by Booker T. Washington! Hot DAMN!!! My family was in college in 1908 and they don't believe in stopping after a master's degree; they always wanted more. So yes, if I do go back to school or if my girls walk around with science books it' because it is in our gene pool. Not weird. Not crazy. Just brilliant! Not many people can say that!

I've been singing every Sunday since my aunt Phyliss challenged us to do something in honor of her mother who would have been 99 years old in 2017. I sing with a whole new conviction. I've met relatives in my first family who had similar first husband stories. I knew I had relatives in my forever family who had similar husbands. Now that fact is a little scary but I look at their second husbands as men who LOVE their wives and aren't afraid to show it or to let you know.

I've used these men as examples for my daughters to know that there are good men out there. By the same token, I don't want them to listen to the media or their friends encouraging them to get married early. There is no rush.

I'd been running into these loving, second-time married folks. I decided that the only way to get back into the swing of dating was to take a leap and dive in. I went back on Match.com. My first and only match a year and a half earlier, showed me that I was worth it. I learned a lot from that guy. Even though I went through hell and back again, I was finally beginning to say it's time to take some time for me and not feel guilty about it. I also learned how to be home alone and enjoy it. I learned to be cautious on dates and from our first meeting, he told me everything I needed to do before I went out with anyone else. Not that he was pushing or brushing me off but he sized me up and said someone needs to know who you're with and where you are as you do this online thing. Together he and I became friends and helped each other rebuild trust in areas we both had doubts. From there we realized we were best working together as friends.

I went out with a few other guys who remained in the friend category. About a month later, I met a couple of other folks who met their significant other online. In talking to my cousin who is a professional matchmaker many of the agencies who do this type of thing use the same sort of basic profile matchmaking algorithm. I looked at guys who had a profile and compared their matches to mine. I had already experienced what it was like to be with someone opposite me, so I questioned would I even like someone who had a lot in common with me? I decided that since I'm not an expert, I needed to take the risk. What I was doing over the past few years wasn't working, which meant I needed to try something new.

23

Second Time Around

My first date with Steven happened after a long talk with God. The Fisher Girls and I were sharing our stories of how to weed out guys and avoid wasting time with online dating. I was giving this online thing one more shot and I was ready to commit to putting in real effort. I decided that I wasn't ready for a relationship, but was open to seeking companionship without the B.S. Early on, Steven made it really easy when he said he forgot he was going on vacation with his boys after he scheduled our first date. *This is B.S.! How do you forget you are going on vacation when you scheduled a date with me? Are you kidding me?* As you can imagine, Steven was weeded out. What's funny is that my aunt had advised me to make a few dates in one day. If I had taken her advice, then I wouldn't have been disappointed.

I shared my dilemma with my cousins and Kelli the matchmaker said, "Joi haven't you ever forgotten plans you made, missed, or almost missed?" Before I could respond, cousin MeChale shared her stories of missed vacations. Then Christie chimed in with a similar story. Nicole and I started laughing about all of our missed appointments. Kelli said, "Maybe you should consider rescheduling." Kelli and MeChale continued talking about things to consider for the next time. If he cancels again, that is a testament to his character, so weed him out.

My cousins' advice sent me back to the room. I plopped on the bed and sent Steven a message. I already had a message typed out and ready to send, but they summoned me to the kitchen because I was spending too much time in the room on the phone with him during our "First Cousins Reunion." Steven and I had been communicating for a week.

We rescheduled our date and since then, I have never been happier. We had a wonderful dinner at my favorite Buffalo Wing spot in South Jersey. The conversation flowed and he expressed his love of family and we had several similar interests. Then I was blown away by his passionate kiss, which erased the thought of going on any other dates. Deep down, I knew that this was the beginning of something special.

In my quiet moments with Steven, he often asks me what's on my mind. I have a whirlwind of thoughts and emotions as I'm taking in our moments together. I was beginning to feel that my lack of responses to his questions that seem simple may make him question if our relationship is going to work. I'm not sure what I feel. Is it self-sabotage? Is it fear? I can't fully explain why it is so difficult for me to answer some of his most basic questions about my thoughts.

As a man whose job often includes confronting issues, I know that my lack of responses can be confusing and probably frustrating. I don't intentionally withhold my response. I'm still trying to figure him out. Do you really want me to respond? I don't sugar coat things and I'm at the point where if my honest answers to his questions turn into an argument, I'M DONE! I know that sharing my experiences takes me to a dark place. I avoid telling him those stories that impact my thoughts, my dreams, or my mood because they are triggers to a host of negative memories.

Of course, I know that for our relationship to succeed, I must give Steven an

opportunity to understand where I am coming from, so I have to share my journey. Writing is my release; it frees my thoughts and allows me to thoughtfully craft many things I have a hard time saying. Writing gives me an opportunity to share thoughts uninterrupted, without wondering what he may be thinking if I were to say these things directly to him or anyone else. Writing allows me to rephrase thoughts that are filled with profanity into words that are politically correct. Everything Steven does is intentional. I hope that as he reads my story, it will help him understand me.

Throughout this journey, Steven hasn't been asking me much about it. He shared with his mom and colleagues at work that I was writing a book but he couldn't even tell them what it was about. It's interesting how he handles me. I often tell him that in my past experience with an argumentative person who emphatically believed that only his opinion counted, to forgive me in advance if he asks me something and I don't respond. There are times when I'm just waiting for Steven's switch to flip and exhibit behaviors that I don't recognize. For the most part, I don't elaborate on things with him even when he asks specific questions. The past couple of months I have been in prayer because we have had some long periods of time apart in our long distance relationship. Once his car was stolen and I was beginning to feel like our conversations were stagnant. Lord knows I appreciate a good conversation and laughter. It was just recently when he finally asked me question after question about the book. At first, I was like, *do I really answer this or do I just kind of answer it because he's not going to listen?* He was asking and waiting for me to respond and elaborate. He sounded attentive and I'm finding that weird but good. Then he shared a few things going on in his life with his children. I said to myself, *thank you God you knew I needed him to turn the corner and be more open with his family conversation.*

In my head, I was thinking, *why did he ask me all these questions today?* I can't say he wasn't listening because he asked several follow up questions. But God you had already revealed to me when I met him that he is very attentive and caring. I have to keep reminding myself that Steven is not *him*. How am I going to get past that? Again, I'm saying all this in my mind as I am not courageous enough to ask him. Then I hear my bosses voice, "Joi ask the damn question!" "What made you go there today with your questions? You never ask me anything about my adoption journey or my past relationship. All this new family and my feelings?"

Before I could finish he said, "Think back to the times that I have asked you things about your family and relationships and you'd say you weren't ready to talk about it or not now. My thought was you would say something when you were ready. But girl trying to crack you open is like next to impossible! But here you are with a book coming out and you are about to be very busy. I need you to know that I am here for you. I know you have some challenges opening up, but I want to know what's going on. I want to be there for you. I want you to know that I'm not going anywhere. I'm here for you Babe. Whatever you need, whatever you say, I got you Joi but you have to let me be there for you. I know some of your past experiences weren't good. I'm trying to get you to open up and you are SLOWLY doing it. But Babe you've got to meet me halfway. I don't know everything about adoption, reunions, or your past relationship, I do want you to know if you think my going to group with you will help me and help us, then I'm willing to do whatever it is we need to do for us."

AWWW I love this man! God, you keep revealing to me why you placed him in my life. Now just reveal all that to my Dad, LOL. Anyone coming into a relationship with me after my last relationship has had to fight through the wall with my family and friends. None of them are allowing any drama-filled folks to latch on to me. My Dad's guard is still up. Lord work on him for me, please. Help build their relationship. I know my dad is going to love Steven, eventually!

One year later, Steven is everything that I hoped for and more. My thoughts waver between, *Are we moving too fast? Why am I resisting if it feels right? This isn't a good look in front of my girls when he visits often.* On the flip side, I miss him when he's not around. *Can we deal with each other on a regular basis? What are we doing? I'm not taking care of no man, been there done that! Can I do an Oprah and Stedman— life partners? Do I really want to get married? Can a person with a six-year itch be in a committed relationship or is this just how he feels right now?* Sometimes I'm afraid that too much consistency may lead to me losing myself. I love Steven and I'm happy to be in a committed relationship. We got engaged on February 1, 2019, at my favorite Sushi restaurant. Steven shared the news with his family and his children. Seven of our eight children reached out to congratulate us— yes that's more than *The Brady Bunch*. Number eight, the youngest of the crew was busy playing video games so Steven planned to catch up with him when he got back to Philadelphia to explain what this all means.

I am in awe at what God is doing and I look forward to finally being happy and at peace in my life. But no matter what, at the end of the day, I know beyond a shadow of a doubt that the joy that I have the world didn't give it to me and world can't it away!

> *"So, no matter what I say, what I believe, and what I do,*
> *I'm bankrupt without love.*
> *Love never gives up.*
> *Love cares more for others than for self.*
> *Love doesn't want what it doesn't have.*
> *Love doesn't strut,*
> *Doesn't have a swelled head,*
> *Doesn't force itself on others,*
> *Isn't always "me first,"*
> *Doesn't fly off the handle,*
> *Doesn't keep score of the sins of others,*
> *Doesn't revel when others grovel,*
> *Takes pleasure in the flowering of truth,*
> *Puts up with anything,*
> *Trusts God always,*
> *Always looks for the best,*
> *Never looks back,*
> *But keeps going to the end."*
> ***1 Cor. 13:4-7 (MSG)***

24

Letters to My Girls

Oftentimes, when people didn't know my name they described my physical features, "You know, the tall lady with the three girls!" For those who have known me for a lifetime, like my sorority sister Regin, she dubbed us "Joi and the Joyettes." During my graduate studies at Kean, my colleague Dion would say, "Here comes Joi and her girls." During that time, my girls were ages 3, 6, and 8. I had to set them up at a table in the back of the classroom until their dad got off of work. They knew they had to work while we worked. Dion still talks about me coming to my college class with three little girls. When he tells this story, he laughs at the reaction of our classmates on the first day. The girls knew they had to do their homework, eat their snack and whisper to one another.

It was because of their ability to be respectful, responsible, quiet and to realize at a very young age that sometimes they had to do something for someone else, even if it wasn't fun for them. They knew mommy believed school was important. It was times like those that I could truly see that what I was pouring into my children as it related to manners, etiquette, responsibility, respect, work ethic, time management and more was all paying off. They were witnessing their mom exhibit all of those characteristics right before their eyes.

As an only child, and then transitioning to a mother of two, I anticipated raising children was more of a cookie cutter approach. I intended to raise my children with the core values that I was raised with; my rules were the rules and the kids would be pretty much the same. I was determined not to raise my kids with some of the fears. I wanted them to enjoy scary movies, not fear cats, and walk into a room and start talking to folks.

Once Traci was born, life quickly showed me that there was no cookie cutter approach. I was in shock that these two human beings came from the same parents. *How difficult and different could baby number two be?* Then life happened. What worked for Jasmin was not going to work with Traci. Then three years later Tasha came along. *Oh Lord, you made them all completely different!* I thought I was armed with information having had two children, but Tasha brought a whole new set to my mommy learning curve. Prior knowledge helped, but they were each their own being and I had to focus and handle each one differently.

I've had the opportunity to watch them grow, watch them screw up, watch them do things beyond my wildest dreams. I've watched them perform, speak publicly, read their published works, and had a front row seat to their meltdowns. I recently heard two of them give their perception of their childhood and my parenting. Both girls said I am like my father in that I talk to others about how proud I am of what they are doing, yet I don't let them know that I see their hard work, and who they are becoming as young women. I was in SHOCK. *ARE YOU KIDDING ME?* I have hooked them up with employment opportunities, and gigs. I refer people to them and I could not believe that they did not think that spoke volumes about my confidence in them. By now, I thought they all knew that I won't cosign my name to anyone I don't believe in.

So before I got mad, I had to reflect and ask myself, *when was the last time I told them I was proud of them and was I specific in my statement?* Then I realized that I had not specifically said it to them in the manner I want things said to me. So I apologized and owned that as something I plan to get better at doing. They often want to know what I think. At times, as parents, we think our expressions of love and loving acts demonstrate to our children that we know we are proud of them. But they have shown me that it's not enough. So to the world, I believe my girls are hardworking, amazing young women, who are beautiful on the inside and out. I am extremely proud that God has placed them in my care.

I am very proud of the good, the bad, and the ugly. If in the bad and the ugly, they see their mishaps, learned something and are working to improve themselves, then I am on board. These past six years have been difficult for ALL of us. I am thankful that we are in a better place mentally and emotionally, yet there is work to be done but I don't want another day to go by without my girls knowing that even as children, they were making moves in life that made me proud.

Dear Jasmin,

As my oldest and first born, I thank you for a lifetime of things and I apologize for a lifetime of first time parenting mistakes. Some were funny and some were not so funny. You have been my right hand and my support throughout times when you should have been able to just be a kid like your sisters. But since you were the oldest, with that comes a lot of responsibility, and you did a great job. While I can say that's the story of the oldest child, I must admit some of these burdens should not have fallen on you. You've come to our aid more than a time or two. I love you for your sacrifice and hope that your growth and development will lead you to step out on faith too.

You have the gifts to organize and plan events and be the life of the party too. Your welcoming of others, a leader, a protector, and your sisters would say a little bossy too. You can sing, dance, and there is an amazing writer in you. I can't wait for you to let God's will be done in your life so we can see him work through you. You had a little tiny voice when you were younger and now your voice comes booming through. Always willing to give your opinion, always willing to give advice, not always open to listening, as you often thought what we were saying just wasn't very nice. I'm never going to tell you something to hurt you, but I'm also not going to yes you to death to be friends with you. I pray that you select a good five folks to surround yourself with because I know God is about to use you. You are competitive and I heard you say it just the other day, "It's time to get it together because my sisters are leading the way!" I love that you push each other and encourage each other. I'm excited about what you've done in life and I'm super excited about what you are going to do. WE can't even envision it. WE don't know His plan. The love you desire in your life is truly in God's hands.

As I enter this new relationship knowing my worth and with fresh eyes too I want you to see that love is patient, love is kind, and love doesn't hurt. Unkind words and false accusations are not a sign of unconditional love. I hope WE paint a better picture and be a better example of how two people in love support, care, encourage, disagree and argue or debate with one another. Six years ago you made a phone call that no child should ever have to make and that was a 911 phone call. I apologize for not having the courage to change our lives sooner. I applaud you for standing up and saying, "I love you and Mommy, I'm not leaving you!"

I am also determined to help you get life back on track to further your education and get your teaching certification. You once again came to help me when our small school couldn't fill a vacancy. In life, you loved being the big sister, the one the others had to look up to, but with that position also came sacrifices. You are bold, you are brave, you are smart and beautiful too. I need you to stop, take a step back, and acknowledge all that we've been through. You are a helper, a protector, a planner, and ventriloquist too. People really thought Traci couldn't talk because you never let her get her words out. Your desire to make sure people feel included, that they are loved, and save the world at the same time are a joy to watch. Right now, I'm hopeful that you will put Jasmin first and allow us to support you. You've always wanted to be grown, but you now know it's overrated. It's time that you allow someone to help you. That's all we've ever wanted to do. That choice is yours.

Love,
Ma

Dear Traci,

As a baby people used to get freaked out by your stare. You had big eyes and you would hold a fixed intense stare as if you could see through them. You made people uncomfortable, the young and the old. It was hilarious because I had no control. I could twist you and turn you and it didn't matter what I tried to do, you kept your eyes on them until you decided you were through. I told people it was a sign of great intuition to come and that one day this was going to be a great resource for you. It's really coming in handy in your dating life and business.

I'm waiting for you to see what the rest of us sees in you. You a beautiful person inside and out and yes your beauty is different from your sisters and that is okay. You each have your own unique look with similarities, (whether you think so or not). But your beauty is beyond your exterior and I need you to get that is a major part about you. "The who do you look like game" is something that people generally do. As a kid, you didn't understand why people picked your face apart in front of you. You wanted a clear delineation of what people saw in you, you didn't want to hear that you looked like a combination of the two. Dr. Lerner said it best after the eye examinations. "You have an eye like your mother and an eye like your father. Your mixture goes down to your eyes too. Once you got to college there was no longer a doubt in anyone's mind, "You look like your mom, YES YOU DO!"

You are competitive but you won't say it out loud. You love working with kids and adults. I love that you are working on your relationship with God and it comes through in everything that you do. Your journey is truly amazing. Stop comparing yourself to "Insta-Trainers!" Your work and worth are not the same. You are an Exercise Scientist, a strength and conditioning coach, you've studied kinesiology, biology, psychology and more. You are a health and fitness guru, a professional developer, a group facilitator, and a life coach. Your time is coming. You've been on a faith-walk in establishing your business. You give back with your time and money. You participate in and support youth in our community. Be patient, God is not through with you yet.

You are good at what you do and you get results. Know your worth. Get ready to fight for your rights in a male-dominated industry. Your creative juices will flow. Your networking skills have improved. Everyone will soon know your name; I feel it in my bones. You have a heart for people and it will pay off in this industry. It's not easy being an entrepreneur but you have your hand in God's hand continue to be lead by Him.

Love will come. God is working on the man for you and I already know he needs to open doors, pull out chairs, put on your coat, love your family, play games, have fun dancing and singing, even if he can't. I see you watching US. You pronounced your love for Steven even before I was willing to and you were constantly reminding me that I was loveable and that I deserve to be treated like this when his kindness and helpful spirit felt weird because I kept waiting for his crazy side to surface. I pray that in my new relationship I am a better example of showing you the love that's in store for you. God's got your back.

Love,
Mom

Dear Tasha,
As I am a the end of writing this book and actually trying to write about you and your sisters, you have come in my room fifty thousand times oblivious to the fact that I have three binders on my bed, a book bag, a bed desk, and I'm on my laptop. That speaks truth to who you are. When you have something you are trying to do you have to get your thoughts out before you forget it, so you will stop everyone from anything they are doing. You speak of rhyming too much in this song you are writing and I share that I just had that experience while I was writing letters. I shared with you that as I listen to music I've learned there are rhymes but that there are also short stories being told. "So what is the song about?" I asked. "Well, it's kind of all over the place." I wanted to say, "OH REALLY? Who would have guessed that?"

When people ask, "What is Tasha up to?" I ask if they want the current version or the version of a month ago. In the end, everything you do falls under the umbrella of the arts and I love that. You have a creative, outgoing, strike while the iron is hot, let's get it done, "what's the worst that can happen," and a competitive spirit.

I don't know if you realize that many of the risks I've taken, I've taken because of one of your random thoughts that always start with, "You know Mommy, you should…" It's been everything from singing more often, take this job I found for you, get back into modeling, write a book, design your own t-shirts, start a podcast or blog, try public speaking and so much more. You are always planting a seed and trying to make me think differently. But there is definitely one suggestion that I will not be taking you up on and it doesn't even spark my interest: Steven and I will **not** *be taking a nude couples picture as models for some master art class. NOT HAPPENING! A bonding experience you say. Only you would seriously recommend that.*

Here you are back in my room again. You say you figured out your song. I'm glad to see you taking your gift of music seriously. I remember when you were four and unfortunately you told everyone that you all got pulled over by the police, and in the same breath you said one day you were going to sing songs with cuss words. Who says that? I was ready to kill your father. He realized at the time that he had to limit the music he played around you because you sure blurted that out at a family event. Years later, you went to a girl band tryout with your sisters. They were looking for a vocalist and you were only about five but could sing so you and your sisters auditioned. When Kimberly's mom brought you out of the room she said, "Tasha played the piano and sang." I responded, 'Tasha played the piano?" She replied, "Yes, Tasha said she had a song she wanted to share and she sat down at the piano and played it." I looked at the lady and said, "She has never had a piano lesson. Are you sure it was Tasha who played the piano'" I knew people get you and your sisters' names mixed up. "Yes, the little one with the dress on. She played and did a very nice job and then sang her song." I told your grandmother that your father and I had been ignoring the clues because you played the piano every day. I remember she said, "Getting the other two to practice was like pulling teeth." It's funny, your sisters could care less about the piano but they were the ones I signed up for lessons thinking that you were too young.

So that's when I enrolled you at the Soumas Heritage School of Music and you made your way to Rose's Music Studio where your foundation and skills were developed. I was proud when you continued on to the Mason Gross youth division. I knew you loved music when on your very last music recital you cried because it was over. You had gotten very competitive with sports, money was tight, and paying for and missing rehearsals was not an option, so you finished your season with Mason Gross and focused on sports and academics. But it was your tears that let me know that it was not the end of music for you.

I knew you began writing songs and making tracks late in high school and in college. Then when the pageant activity began again that was the first time in years that I heard you sing all out. The music industry is a challenging industry but you have the talent, you have the ear, you have the writing ability to craft your thoughts and feelings into interesting lyrics. It is my hope that as you discover yourself as an artist and that you don't compromise who you are to fit the narrow platform that women of color are given. You have to determine what you want your brand to be and not be branded by what other folks say is the thing that sells.

Ratchetness and ignorance may get you noticed or starting a beef with a female musician might get you fifteen minutes of fame, but at the end of the day, only those with real talent will have the longevity for a lasting respectful career. You've got brains, creativity, talent, and beauty. God didn't bring you this far in life to reduce yourself to something else less than to fit in. He's going to find a place for you and your sick beats, girly attitude, and proper way of speaking. That sweatshirt I gave you said, "Pretty, Black, and EDUCATED" and God is going to use all that as He works through you. Keep hustling, planning, networking, learning, trying new things, promoting, marketing, blogging, writing, singing, playing, TEACHING :-), dancing, collaborating, sharing, exercising, praying, styling, loving, managing, and just doing all the things that you desire to do.

Your experiences are helping you narrow down the things you definitely want to do. Keep trusting that if it's God's will, it will be achieved. AND you just came BACK in my room standing there staring at me through the crack of the door insisting that I stop to take a break to eat because that would make me more productive. Of course, you add that you are pretty sure I've said that to you before.

Glad you are back home. Glad you are figuring out life. Oh, and yes please forgive us for leaving you home the day your sisters got baptized. I thought he had you and he thought I had you and after the Baptism of your sisters, we realized no one had you. While you were home you said you cried and eventually got a bowl and made yourself some cereal and watched Barney. I now connect that act to your need to always know where everyone is when you are in the house. I get it. I apologize it was in our rushing around I would never just up and leave you. I love you too much for that.

And for you, love will come. God is still working on you before he can bring someone He sees fit. Be patient. Don't settle. You are loveable. You have a good heart. And NO do not follow my lead and marry young. And as I told you, "If he's trying to get your attention by telling you that you're cute, tell him you are glad to see his eyes work!" If you haven't found your five people in your camp of support lets get on it. You've got work to do. Let's get it right.

Love
Mommy

I am more than honored and blessed that God has chosen me to be your mom. Thanks to you all, my life has been filled so much love, laughter, and incomprehensible joy. The best of our infinite new beginnings is yet to come! Find your village. Love yourself. And most of all, find your JOY!

Acknowledgments

For my girls, Jasmin, Traci and Tasha, my reason for being, even in the times of chaos you bring me joy! You each sacrificed and silently struggled along this journey, but as MeChale says 'Baby, you should not look like your story!' and we surely do not. God has been so good to us and through it all, WE are of sound mind, body, and soul and we ought to tell somebody how we made it. I thank GOD for each of you!

Jasmin, you are an awesome talent. Your gifts as a writer, planner, counselor, an aspiring teacher, coupled with a determined spirit are bubbling under the surface. I can't wait to see how those gifts manifest in your life. Don't give up! It's time to turn it up a notch.

Traci you are caring, a forward-thinker, and you have a desire to serve people. Your intuition is a gift from God. Lean on Him, Trust in Him, God is going to open doors for Sculpted Turtle Fitness that will be greater than anything you can imagine. BEAST MODE!

Tasha you are a fearless, creative, networker, and planner. All of this experience is a blessing. YES, you are all over the place, but God will reel you in and set you on the path that He has for you. Keep hustling and learning! Your hard work will pay off. Producer, blogger, social media strategist, musician and yes, teacher your skills benefit any business.

To my Mom who said forget about folks feelings and write the book! I thank you for your years of encouragement when I didn't believe in myself. Thanks for challenging me with your reverse psychology. You demonstrate unconditional love each and every day!

To my Dad who brought every adoption news article to my mailbox for over ten years, made me do presentations when I needed money for something, and challenged me to think of things from all perspectives when making decisions. Thank you for your never-ending love and support.

Thanks, Uncle Lee and Aunt Joanne, Uncle Harold and Aunt Terri, Uncle Charles* and Aunt Carolyn, Uncle George* and Aunt Rosetta,* and Aunt Elinda,* you all have played a role in my life and upbringing. You ALL helped me and the girls along the way. The VILLAGE.

To Kisha Hebbon, Esq. and in memory of Dr. Waymon Benton,* you both reminded me that one day my story of survival would be helpful to someone else and this craziness would make a great book. To Christian Wellness Center and Danielle Jean Pierre, you redirected me to Christ and reminded me NOT to be ashamed of my story. To Kim Rouse an amazing and inspiring talent who brought this work to life. A brilliant mind, beautiful spirit, and infectious energy. I'm forever grateful for what you've done and what you are about to do! The BEST is YET to come.

To Pat, Flora and John thank you. This book was written before this adoption reunion began and these new experiences and understandings of self-changed the trajectory of my life and this work. Thanks for LIFE! Thanks, Aunt Eileen for saying "We always knew about you!" a statement adoptees hope for. Thanks, Aunt Lois for saying, "There is no denying you, you've got our legs!" and for sharing your journey with me. Thanks for sharing that you loved reading your anatomy book, Traci then realized her love of science wasn't weird because doctors run in her family. Thanks, Aunt Lillian for inspiring me through your work and demonstrations of love as a caregiver. Thanks, Aunt Phyllis for the photo album, family tree, and MEDICAL HISTORY!!

To all the NJCARE Advocates and Pam Hasegawa you never gave up and WE are grateful. My life and relationships are forever changed. To

Governor Christie, Senator Joseph Vitale and Senator Diane Allen, former Assemblywoman Sheila Oliver, and all of the political supporters of the NJ Birthright Act, OUR LIVES ARE FOREVER CHANGED. Thank you for fighting for us. To all my support group members. You validate my concealed perception of feeling different, misunderstood, out of place, and weird. I now know those thoughts are NORMAL adoptee issues. To the birth parents and adopted parents in our groups THANK YOU for your openness and honesty as we get to hear honest thoughts on your fears, questions, and things you long for as you deal with your child in reunion.

Thanks, ICA for offering counseling and support services for adoptees, for running groups, and for your support. Thank you, Damon Davis, for being the brainchild behind Who Am I Really podcast. You give adoptees and other members in the adoption triad an opportunity to share their story in a supportive way and you archive our stories for others to listen to. Special thanks to Maurice Daniel for stopping to have a good old conversation with Damon while traveling for this connection to come about. YES, put down the phones young people, talk to people.

To Pastor Thomas, Rev. Thorpe, Pastor Soaries, Rev. Keenan, and Pastor Miller, your sermons encouraged me, inspired me, soothed my soul, and challenged me during my darkest days.

To my three: Alexia, Yolanda, and Nicole. My voices of reason, my give it to you straight, my, "Joi you cannot say that!", "Joi you got this!," "Joi this room is a mess," or even "I'm proud of you!" Whatever I needed, you all were there in your own way. It never matters how much time has passed you got me! To IB Spg '92, the Fisher Girls, Alstons, thanks for being there for me in the past, present and the future. To the authors in my family and several family friends Baruti Kafele & Dr. Tannis as educators and authors, you all inspired me. Love you ALL. To my friend Ms. Enjolica from EJay Photography thanks for being there for all of us from me to the grandbaby. Photojournalist and friend, you captured moments I could never repeat. THANK YOU! To Ringo, John and Doug thanks for reminding me to take care of me, to Live, Love, and Laugh, and special thanks for being available as stand up, reliable men in the lives of my girls. To the Ladies of Delta Sigma Theta Sorority, Inc., my colleagues at Jefferson, Hubbard, Evergreen, PHS (Cardinals), PHS (Chiefs), the UG and the Ladies of Phi Delta Kappa Sorority, Inc. for your dedication to the community and children.

Special thanks to my former staff at **Maxson** where I served as Acting Principal and former staff at **UC TEAMS** where I served as High School (HS) Principal and eventually HS and K-8 Principal ... we had exciting times, tough times, fun times, and times where I was so exhausted I called myself to the office on the loudspeaker :-). Through it all, your hard work and laughter kept me afloat when you could not imagine what was going on in my life outside of school. In memory of Bettie Quinn and Gertie Edmondson two women who encouraged reading, writing, and creativity. Laughter meant more to me than any of you will ever know. To my brothers and .5 at the EMPIRE (JL, Ritchie, JB and TE), to our Deans (Brunson, Rogers, Calvo, Eyler, McGowan), and Miriam thanks for your support and teamwork through tough times when you were just being a team player not knowing I didn't know how I was going to make it through the day. To DDW and WFB thanks for giving me a safe space to share my story, for speaking up for me, and for listening. In memory of Linda Jackson thanks for giving me a new opportunity to sing each week and use the gift God has given me. You and your fight for life have been an inspiration!

To my brother John, my twin sisters Camila and Carmela thank you for your kindness. Adding a new sibling with three children and a granddaughter forty six years later is an emotional roller coaster. I thank you for opening your heart. I look forward to getting to know you all.

Thanks Kim, Pam, and Sam for reading and rereading the work. Thanks for making your editing remarks while maintaining my voice.

Special thanks to Dina for sharing information about Miriam's Heart adoption and foster care organization that's right in my backyard (Bridgewater, NJ). Mr. and Mrs. Occhipinti and their executive board are doing AMAZING things. I cried during my meeting with them. I cried on my way home. God laid it on your heart to share information with me about them and I believe this will be my outlet to reach children and families in adoption and foster care.

To Steven, you support me, encourage me, care for me, love me, speak my love language, and accept me as I am. As I was Finding Joi, taking back things that I lost, and changing my thinking. Your last minute date cancellation was not supposed to get you another opportunity at a first date! I was like God, You've Got Jokes! You expect me to believe this man forgot he was going on vacation. Yeah okay. I'm glad I shared that dilemma with The Fisher Girls and I'm glad that I prayed about it and didn't lean on my own understanding. I decided years ago it's time to get out of my own way, pray, and leave it in God's hands. Obedience pays off … Let's see what God has planned for us, He will reveal it. I love you and look forward to being your wife.

Proverbs 3:5 Trust in the Lord with all thine heart and he shall direct thy path. Isaiah 54:17 No weapon formed against me shall prosper.

My final thanks go out to everyone in our VILLAGE - ALL of our friends and family near and far. Here's to life's new journey with new family and friends. We are not subtracting anyone from the fold, just adding on another layer … thanking you in advance for your love, kindness, encouragement, and support. Joi Renee F.A.B.W. for life!

The Apple Doesn't Fall Far From The Tree

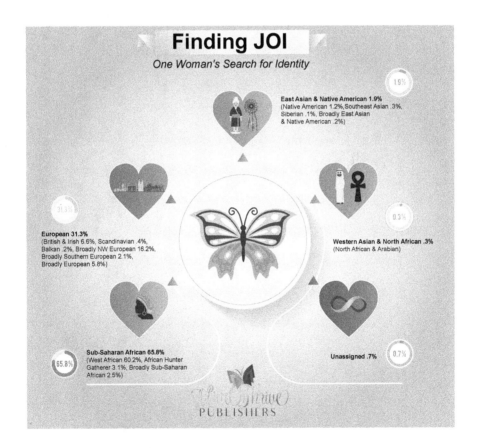

Finding JOI

One Woman's Search for Identity

East Asian & Native American 1.9%
(Native American 1.2%, Southeast Asian .3%,
Siberian .1%, Broadly East Asian
& Native American .2%)

European 31.3%
(British & Irish 6.6%, Scandinavian .4%,
Balkan .2%, Broadly NW European 16.2%,
Broadly Southern European 2.1%,
Broadly European 5.8%)

Western Asian & North African .3%
(North African & Arabian)

Sub-Saharan African 65.8%
(West African 60.2%, African Hunter
Gatherer 3.1%, Broadly Sub-Saharan
African 2.5%)

Unassigned .7%

PUBLISHERS

The Joy Of Great Memories

Reunion with Momma Flo

Aunt Phyllis presented me with a binder of family photos, my family tree, and my MEDICAL HISTORY.

All of her grandparents from my side of the family, Steven and I in the back. LOVE THIS!!

The village; sisters and first cousins coming to check out little cousin.

That family resemblance I had only experienced with my daughters until now. Say CHEESE!

After her testimony she introduced me. Photo by Enjolica
Richardson

My mom is really talking to my birth mom.

All I heard was a lot of thank you's.

My birth mom meets my Dad.

We just pause and embrace.

Now that we stopped crying

They are like bookends. I am now complete.

I'm told agencies worked to find similarities in birth and adopted parents.

A family choir planned for our first extended family gathering.

Sister Sister

Nana with Tasha and my first cousins Shonna and Keisha.

Aunt Tasha, Kami and Jas. Toddlers at a pageant not a good idea.

My Dad meeting my birth mom's matriarch of the family.

Kamryn's First Birthday party!

Trying to take a decent picture of three toddlers was an impossible task.

We all seem to have the same smile.

Auntie couldn't wait to get a hold of Kami. Photo by Tracy Gray

He presented me with my copy of my _____ college degree from _____ signed by Booker T. Washington.

Books as gifts documenting the life's work of Tuskegee Airmen Spann Watson who was a relative.

All of her grandparents from my side of the family, Steven and I in the back. LOVE THIS!!

Poppa John sharing family history. My Dad listening in.

Cousin Pat and Rodney showing us a little hand dancing.

Welcome to Jersey. Meeting my father and Step-Mom.

Papa John and Mildred. He said he was traveling to see his
Granddaughter compete.

My Father and My Dad. This was truly a picture of me being
squished.

Auntie and Uncle another family gathering in D.C.

Our first photo with Poppa John

Mildred couldn't wait to get her hands on the grandbaby.

Tasha's BACK in Atlanta and Aunt Eileen and Uncle Tracy. Luv them

Atlanta family!! What a great welcoming party. Photo by Pam
Hasegawa

Entrepreneurs in the Family! So PROUD of Cousin Erin Gray in
Atlanta, GA

Auntie says "Wait a minute you have to get my good side"

The Doctor is in the House. Dr. Lillian Beard.

Dr. Beard's Wall of Honor with photos with several former Presidents

Jasmin the party planner extraordinaire is getting ready

I was given a relative's diploma signed by Booker T. Washington

Poppa John and Sonja comparing notes

Every activity is a competition

Have you ever… tell me about it I did the same thing before here's my story, sign my sheet please

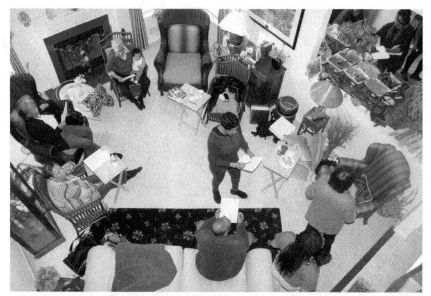

There will be NO sitting around this is Getting to Know You 101

Cousin Pat and Rodney showing us some dance moves

Hand dancing is where they met

Cousin Pat and Rodney showing us their footwork

Pop Pop give them a preview of the song You'll Never Find before the show

Aunt Eileen and my brother John

Joi, John Sr., John Jr. I have a little brother

My Uncle just asked me about my life up to this point. WOW that's a
loaded question.

Welcome to the family luncheon at Auntie's house

Auntie and Cousin Pat who helped put all the pieces together

Around every corner was another relative

Welcome to the family dinner in Maryland.

On the water in Maryland with Poppa John

My Girls

Traci, Tasha, Jasmin at Tasha's Miss Teen New Jersey pageant

Leaving Pop-Pop's favorite breakfast spot ... Perkins.

This summer they got so dark people don't recognize them the first days of school..

Served as a soloist at a family members funeral in Pennsylvania

Rose's Studio Scholarship Luncheon. Tasha's piano presentation.

The village; sisters and first cousins coming to check out little cousin.

Sister Sister

Aunt Tasha, Kami and Jas. Toddlers at a pageant not a good idea.

Jas and Tash twinning.

My favorite picture of the girls. Personality Shot.

Track in the FAMILY!

Our first photo with Poppa John

Gma and the girls as Tasha's piano recital

Love this picture. My mom always found same outfit in different colors.

Come here Sis let's get this sunlight

Tasha's BACK in Atlanta. Auntie and Uncle are happy to see her

Atlanta family!! What a great welcoming party. Photo by Pam
Hasegawa

Pops singing You'll Never Find giving the family a preview of the
Rock and Soul Review

What a CHRISTMAS this was!

Tasha's Cross Country senior night.

Silly selfies at a track meet.

And the LAST has finished High School! % 2016

In our Sunday Best!

Family and Friends day 2017!

Beach life featuring TeeTee and Kami

TeeTee and Kami is her crib.

When Aunt Tasha and Kami go to the mall, they ride unicorns.

How much of each ancestry did you inherit from your parents? Connect a parent on 23andMe to see what ancestries you inherited from each parent. Or, connect with your children so they can see what you passed down to them. Learn more about the benefits of connecting.

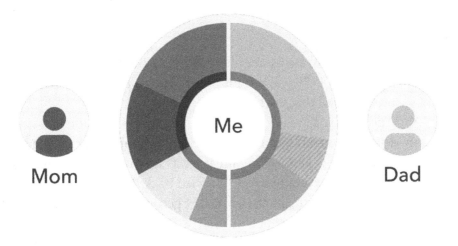

Adoption Timeline

Joi Renee Fisher

Some of the first questions people ask are: 1) Do you know why you were adopted? When people ask me this question, they hesitate to say "given up" and their voices tend to trail off. 2) Do you know why your parents didn't have children? 3) Have you always wanted to know? 4) What lead you to your search? 5) How did it all begin? 6) Where are you now with everything?

- ❖ Always knew I was adopted. (Photo album with card) Also knew June 1970 was an important date in that my parents received me at that time
- ❖ Adopted by a great loving family, but always felt different
- ❖ 1984 Art exhibit at Plainfield High School. Security guards and students kept asking me if I was in one of the pictures in the library art showcase. I modeled back then and there was a girl in African print attire with a tiger who appeared to be my identical twin.
- ❖ 1988 Graduated from HS. (Going to college too much stress to do search now)
- ❖ 1992 Graduated from College (Job searching and too much stress to do a search now)
- ❖ 1993 Birth of Jasmin, 1st Child (need for medical information) and planning a wedding
- ❖ 1994 Getting Married

- ❖ 1995 Birth of Traci, 2nd Child (greater need for medical information) contacted Adoption agency and purchased non-identifying information. Debate Sheriff's Officer or Teacher
- ❖ 1996 Teaching to present time (Busy schedule...NO TIME)
- ❖ 2011 Friend and colleague mentions success with DNA on Ancestry.com
- ❖ 2013
  - ➢ All Year my father provided all published articles about adoption laws changing. He put them in my mailbox.
  - ➢ Separation
  - ➢ 2nd Child off to college. While on overnight visit heard TV commercial for 23andme
  - ➢ Life in pure chaos
  - ➢ Leaving a large local district as Asst. Principal to small local charter where I am a Founder to become Principal taking a $10k+ salary reduction that I didn't tell my family about
- ❖ 2014
  - ➢ Still receiving all published articles about adoption laws changing from my father in my mailbox.
  - ➢ Little to no minority matches on 23andme
- ❖ 2015
  - ➢ Still receiving all published articles about adoption laws changing from my father in my mailbox.
  - ➢ May 3rd Found 1st Cousin Shiva on 23andme
  - ➢ May 5th After I mentioned adoption, no further emails from Shiva
  - ➢ Decided to try online dating
  - ➢ Turned to Ancestry - Greater chance of finding minority matches
- ❖ 2016
  - ➢ Still receiving all published articles about adoption laws changing from my father in my mailbox.

- June
  - June 1st Start new job at large local district as Asst. Principal. A job my daughter Jasmin discovered for me
  - June 23rd Message to 1st to 2nd Cousin Pat Frye
  - June 25th dropped adoption bomb
  - June 25th Message to 1st to 2nd Cousin Loretta - no response
- August Invited to Frye family reunion in Virginia (Declined I had just started a new job in June)
- September no matches from cousin Pat. I told Pat about the upcoming law changes
- Article given to me about Original Birth Certificate (OBC) applications in late 2016
- November
  - Applied for OBC
  - Told my boss about challenges with my Ex as I hear he had been making his rounds to my friend's homes. Still talking crazy
- December both parents on the same day gave me the same OBC article to read
- ❖ 2017
  - Jan
    - Jan 8th Message from Pat "Any news yet"
    - Emailed NJCARE regarding legislation celebration and luncheon
    - Jan 9th Attended event at the state department
    - Jan 11th Received OBC
    - FB Messenger & Mailed letters
    - Jan 29th birth mom contacted me and gave me birth father's name
    - Jan 29th birth father called me
  - Feb
    - 2nd Sat, First NJCARE Meeting
    - Sat/Sun Speed Reading books on Reunions

- Feb. 12th, 2nd Sun, Met Birth Mother at church
- 4th Sun, Combined family + birth family. Met extended family
> March
  - 2nd Sat, Met Birth Father
  - 2nd Sun, Found out my Mom has lung cancer
  - 4th Sat, Family and Birth mother and father attended a concert my father and I performed in.
  - March 31, birth mom Flo's Birthday
> April
  - April 1st Panelist with NJ CARE at conference @ Rutgers Univ. I learned how big the adoption world and conferences are.
  - April 7th Joi's birthday (Given two of my birth grandmothers bracelets as a gift)
  - April 9th Mom's birthday
  - April 10 - 13th One on one with Birth mother at her home
  - April 20th Mom has surgery
  - April 22nd Met NJ CARE Post legislative team. Shared story
> May
  - May 5th Birth mom comes to stay with me at Father's house, attends dance concert at work and girls track meet
  - May 6th Birth mom joins me at church
  - May 12th 2nd Child (Head, Heart, High incident)
  - May 13 & 14th 2nd Child (Back at the hospital)
  - May 13th Share journey with Sorority during announcements
  - May 14th Mother's Day
  - May 15 & 16 2nd Child Heart monitor
  - May 27th Birth mother's huge Memorial Day Cookout. Meeting full extended family and friends

➤ June
  ▪ June 3 -4th Meet Birth father's extended family and friends. Meet brother (website picture versus reality)
  ▪ June 10th NJ CARE Support Group
  ▪ Found out article I am featured in by Tina Kelley was given the green light from NJ Monthly magazine for October publication
  ▪ June 11th Asked to sing last minute solo. Thoughts of backing out. FB Msg from Phyliss - Do something in honor of mom who would have been 99. Mentioned she loved singing gospel music out loud, flowers. Did not have a choice but to say YES to the solo given that challenge
  ▪ June 18th Father's Day
  ▪ June 21st Beach day with Birth mom and older two girls + grand
  ▪ June 27th Mom started chemo
  ▪ June 30th Who Am I Really? Podcast
➤ July
  ▪ Attending National Adoption Conference in Atlanta
  Pam, NJ CARE Adoption Advocate is receiving an award for her life's work as an advocate
  ▪ We are staying with my birth father's sister's home in Atlanta
  ▪ Pam, NJ CARE Advocate will get to meet my birth family. Some of my family and friends may be able to attend.
  ▪ First Cousins Reunion in Texas after hearing some success stories I decided to put some effort into online dating
➤ August and September
  ▪ Spent a lot of time being sick
  ▪ I told some and reminded others ALL my family that from September - October, I drop off the face of the

other with all the start of school events. I used to try to do everything.

- Met my Match. Told my line sister the next day at a cookout "I found my O." Her husband's name starts with an O and he is an amazing man. Closed my online account. They warned me to be careful and not rush.

➤ October
  - "Church seems to be very important to you would you mind if I come one Sunday?" he said. WHAT?? I've never been asked that before.
  - Invited to Movie Premiere on transracial adoption
  - Still sick
  - Started going out with friends. Hanging with the girls.

➤ November
  - My oldest has a baby girl
  - Decided all the Grandma's will need a Gma name so the baby isn't confused. My daughter's side of the family gives my granddaughter NINE grandparents.
  - Became a Grandmother "JoJo"

➤ December
  - Holidays and dealing with splitting my time between the Fisher family and birth family
  - Decided I needed another support group

➤ 2018
➤ January
  - 11th a silent Celebration for ME. This is the one year anniversary of the day I got my OBC in the mail
  - 29th another silent Celebration of communicating with my birth parents
  - Stressed
  - How and when will a relationship be established with my half brother and step-sisters

➤ February
  - 2nd Annual Black History Program at birth mom's church

    First Cousin Preaching
    I'm singing

- Met with Supervisor of Harvest of Hope a former Foster Care agency that was the highest placement agency for black children for several years. Shared my story with her. Shared my desire to figure out how God expects me to use this journey to help others.
- Still having challenges balancing my emotions. Am I angry, sad, happy? Why am I feeling like I'm not sure if I should fully connect? Why do I keep getting thoughts that they are going to leave?

➤ March

- Injured shoulder at work. FURIOUS!!!!
- Three days of PT a week plus doctor's appointments. ANNOYED!! On top of counseling sessions, regular sick visits for sinus infections and allergic reactions.
- Was one of the emcees for my Sorority's Literary Cafe. Renewed my energy to keep writing and editing my book
- Wrote and edited every day
- Paternal Aunt in town for business. Birth mom's bday dinner. How's this gonna go down?
- Felt bad for my boyfriend he is surrounded by Aries women

➤ April

- Told ALL my family April - June I drop off the face of the other with all the start of school events.
- Decided to head over to Phi Delta Kappa Sorority Inc. Epsilon Alpha professional development and was inspired by the special guest my double soror and author. Lead to believe I too could be an author

- Wrote and edited every day

➤ May

- From an empty nest to a full house
- Added another young adult to my household

- Wrote and edited every day
- Asked therapist at the Infertility and Adoption Counseling Center to send me any research papers she had that I could read up on.
- June
  - First road trip blending families. From Jersey to Maryland to North Carolina to Atlanta and back
  - Wrote and edited every day
  - Boat rides with family
  - Reading and highlighting adoption articles
- July
  - He's pissed. I'm pissed. You let him eat all that junk, sorry but this will not mess up my day because you won't listen. Disappointed. Feeling very uncertain. Really all that grease!!!
  - First argument. Realized my triggers are still very heightened. Speechless. Frozen in time. Flashbacks. When does that feeling go away?
  - Enough writing. Revise. Edit.
- August
  - Learning to enjoy the beach with birth family. This really is relaxing
- September - November
  - Lot's of editing and revising
  - Working with designers for t-shirt design for publishing company
  - Stressed. Attending group sessions and individual sessions
  - Working with Sculpted Turtle Fitness on branding
  - Difficulty balancing family. Still struggling
  - In prayer about everything going on
  - Honest conversations - What names do we include? Whose pictures do we use? Who doesn't want to be named?

- What do I do with the little time I have for the holidays with the double the family?
- Talking with potential endorsers. Sharing story updates with them.
- Thinking about the layout for the actual book launch event
- Identifying giveaways, signage, protocol once at the table
- Shared my story with the chairs of our Sorority committee and learned of some other adoption stories. Ordered their friends books and have been reading and highlighting

➢ December
- Tasha annoyed with my lack of presence on social media. She begins to work her magic
- My little cousin passed away in her early twenties and I have been reflecting quite a bit on FAMILY as I didn't really know her.
- Every day and night is a book editing, revising day. I'm also reading all kinds of literature. Who knew this stuff existed?
- Going through the lists of stories needed to fill in gaps where the details might not be clear
- The best Christmas present ever. A consultation with a natural hair expert at Studio Shi Shi. She reviewed all my products and told me what to use and why.
- Are you going to tell it or not tell it? That's the question. "You can't leave the reader hanging Joi" says Kim my book coach. "Now tell me the rest of that story I want to know the details."
- Talking with potential endorsers
- With the LIFT girls I wrote my 25 goals but I'm stuck. I know my goals require work but aren't leaps of faith and they don't include my dreams.

- Do I put his name in the book or don't I? I know he's going to ask me to marry him but as it stands he's a boyfriend. Me and thoughts of relationships and abandonment. Turns into is he in it for the long haul? Are my birth parents in this for the long haul?
- I'm reflecting on a comment my little cousin said a couple years ago about when I went from being their big cousin that took them everywhere to me becoming a mom and seeing very little of them. Time and FAMILY
- Traci's friend asked me 'How has this experience changed your perspective on what FAMILY means?' That's a loaded question and I don't want to try to process my thoughts to answer that.
- Writing until the wee hours of the morning and waking up exhausted. This is an emotional roller coaster.
- Calling on the Village to pick their brains - these are my thoughts on a school curriculum
- Social media following is increasing. Go Tasha
- ❖ 2019
  - ➤ January
    - New Year's Eve reevaluating goals over the past five years. Feeling afraid to write goals for this year so much has changed in my life.
    - Babe what are your goals? Write them down. At the New Year's Eve service Pastor spoke about having setting our goals higher and expecting them to happen. That means being bold enough to write it. Is it okay to say I expect to be married? I really do but that seems so rude or bold to say. I mean he knows I'm not playing house with a boyfriend.
    - Had an amazing conversation with a student whose story has to be told. This reminded me why I want to start the publishing company too. Helping others share their stories is a part of my dream. OK I said it.

- Calling on the Village of authors to pick their brains - Conference Call with MeChale Fisher - Jones author of *Stronger Than the Day Before.*
- Calm, Chaos, and this roaring undercurrent of the reality of this book and all these relationships has me feeling uneasy, afraid, and not able to articulate that
- Every day and night editing, revising, and sometimes writing new ideas.
- Practicing the shingling method I learned for my natural curls. Now I want the world to learn about natural hair care. Not being able to manage my hair was just another thing that made me feel different
- Tasha's pageant and we captured a picture with ALL her grandparents

➤ My birth mom says - We Are ALL In This Together

- Dinner with the my fellow administrators from other districts. No school talk just laughs and catching up. "Are you getting married?" "YES" "She said that confidently" "I feel it coming"
- Silently celebrated January 11th the day I received my OBC
- Family Crisis my daughter called on my birth mom to come in town for support that Friday night. I wasn't going to ask her but I decided all she could do was say NO. I invited her to come to the support group the next day. She said YES.
- Birth mom joined me at NJCARE Support Group
- Working with designers for t-shirt design with book title
- Told my Dad about her visit to the group. Had a great conversation that evening with him about that experience. Have to get him and my mom to read the book 25 Things Adopted Children wish their Adopted Parents Knew. He just does not understand my perspective. He has to come next.

- Told Steven about the support group, told him about the conversation with Dad.
- Working with a designer on the flier
- Steven asked if it would be okay for him to attend a session with me and shares why he thinks it's important.
- Founder's Day an amazing day in the history of Delta Sigma Theta
- Amazing Black Tie affair in honor of NJ Orators with Nor-Jer-Men
  Found my new Favorite Live Band. My dream is to have them for my 50th birthday
- Unhappy with the sample book designs. Found a new designer to work with
- Started a new women's support group at the Christian Wellness Center
- Sorting and formatting pictures is a pain
- Calling on the Village of authors to pick their brains - Conference Call with Kelli K. Fisher author of The MatchMaking Duo
- My daughter and my natural hair whisperer, Tanj, are behind the scenes planning my ponytail and outfit for the event.
- My other daughter is telling me who should do my makeup and what Ms. Ollie should do to my hair. I love having options!
- Calling on the Village of authors to pick their brains - Conference Call with Dr. Lynette Tannis author of Educating Incarcerated Youth
- Signed paperwork for a friend who hopes to adopt
- Back and forth with shirt design
- Participated in Jean Strauss' filming for a documentary on NJ Open Birth Records. My mom and the girls joined me. My support group realized how much my mothers look alike. My mom and girls got to hear other adoptees stories. I learned my mom always wondered

if she should have told me. My friend and advocate, Marty was a late discovery adoptee and he told her she absolutely did the right thing by telling me. I told her I thought she did the right thing too.

- ➤ February
  - Felt like something was going to happen over dinner. He proposed at my favorite restaurant in the Sushi Room. I'm not often speechless. I couldn't eat or talk. I'm ENGAGED!
  - Realized everyone else knew weeks ago that he was going to propose. He was able to ask three of my four parents and my girls without my knowing.
  - Finalized the book cover
  - Conference Calls
  - Working with a designer to design the bookmarks
  - Conversations with Pam regarding a recently published article about DNA
  - I'm struggling telling people I have a book coming out. So I write a little something. When I double back and talk to people everyone is touched by adoption.
  - Just learned of a local group run by a couple and I hear they promote adoption education. I can't wait to check them out. Miriam's Heart in Somerset, NJ
  - Working with designer on templates for presentations
  - Working on captions for pictures
  - Family Crisis
  - Mapping out ideas for the table for the display. AND what am I going to talk about when they hand me the microphone
  - March 30th - Book Launch...Wow

My Confirmation

==

While attending various adoption support groups I learned about all of the different resources and literature on adoption. I also learned that many of these resources are available for free through NJ ARCH. There are workshops and conferences that take place nationally and internationally that I had no idea existed. I never once thought about looking at adoption research until now. As a person who has done all kinds of research papers, why did I never think to check if there was any research out there about adoptees? In hindsight, maybe I didn't because I was blocking out that aspect of my life, thinking that it had no impact. I am so glad of the passing of The Adoptee's Birthright Bill (P.L. 2014, C.9) which has intrigued me enough to ask adoption-friendly counselors and therapist to share articles they've read, because now I am armed with information. There was CONFIRMATION for me in reading the information. It was not out of the ordinary for me to feel out of place, it wasn't weird for me to feel different. I'm not crazy for having these feelings that people won't stick around. I could never explain why I felt that in any relationship that once we had no contact you wouldn't remember me. ALL of it makes sense now... these are adoption issues and natural outgrowths of my situation. Now, I can put these feeling into perspective. I can be open to love, open to connection, and be more certain in understanding my value in another person's life. I believe I am meant to tell my story because there is someone else in the world who needs to know that these are normal adoption issues. CONFIRMATION!! Below you will find highlights from some of the books and/or articles that I've read:

Eggleston, Sarah. *FORMING A SENSE OF SELF: Multiple Choices for Adoptees. Center for Adoption Support and Education,* 2001.

"The most obvious complexity is that adoptees have not one, but two families to consider as they consider what kind of person they would like to be."

"... self-esteem of some young children can be diminished by the conclusions they draw about their adoption."

"It is often assumed that a domestic or same race adoption removes many of the challenges of identity for adoptees. However, unless they have been adopted by relatives, adoptees do not share the same heritage as their adoptive families. Therefore, they are still likely to consider biological make-up, lifestyle, ethnicity, and educational background, as well as other differences they know about when they wonder which parents they resemble."

"As adoptee's self-perception will usually be based on the family and environment in which she has grown up."

"It is preferable that children know the details of their history by the time they enter adolescence. Children need this knowledge to manage the heightened task of identity formation during adolescence."

==

Freedman, Joel. *Notes for Practice An Adoptee in Search of Identity.* **National Association of Social Workers. 2001.**

"It was his desire to know his origins, not out of rejection of his adoptive parents, but as a way of establishing his own identity."

==

Lieberman, E. James. *Adoption and Identity,* **Adoptions Quarterly, 2:2, 1-5, DOI: 10.1300/J145v02n02 01. 1998**

"The popular media still use the dichotomy "Adoptive" vs. "real" parents and adopted

"Adoption, never an accident, ought to be a source of pride and joy like birthing, a celebration of uniquely human parenthood."

"Unfortunately, adoption still reminds most people of biological limitations rather than of human creativity."

"Why even tell a child the truth about his or her adoptions when it is not obvious? I can think of three reasons: (1)so the child won't hear it from someone else; (2) so the parents can deal with questions like "Where was I born?" (3) to get genetic information germane to health."

"... children will have to educate their peers and teachers about what family really means..."

===

Colaner, Colleen Warner; Halliwell, Danielle; Guignon, Phillip. What Do You Stay to Your Mother When Your Mother's Standing Beside You? Birth and Adoptive Family Contributions to Adoptive Identity via Relational Identity and Relational-Relational Identity Gaps. National Communication Association. 2014.

"Grounded in the communication theory of identity, the present study explores how adoptive identity - an individual's understanding of what it means to be an adopted person - is influenced by the relational layer of his or her adoptive and birth family relationships."

"... a person's sense of self is part of his or her social behavior, and the sense of self emerges and is defined and redefined in social behavior." (Hecht, Warren, Jung, & Kreiger, 2005, p260).

===

Gowan, Barbara Ann. *Blending In Crisscrossing the Lines of Race, Religion, Family, and Adoption*. iUniverse. 2007.

===

Engel, Beverly. *The Emotionally Abused Woman Overcoming Destructive Patterns and Reclaiming Yourself.* **Random House Publishing Group. 1990**

Engel, Beverly. *The Emotionally Abused Woman: Overcoming Destructive Patterns and Reclaiming Yourself.* **Fawcett Columbine, 1992.**

"Emotional abuse is like brainwashing in that it systematically wears away at the victim's self-confidence, sense of self-worth, trust in her perceptions, and self-concept." p. 10

"... No matter how successful, how intelligent, or how attractive she is, she still feels "less than" other people. " p. 7

"Effects of emotional abuse - depression, lack of motivation, confusion, difficulty concentrating or making decisions, low self-esteem, feelings of failure, worthlessness, and hopelessness, self-blame, and self-destructiveness but do not understand what is causing these symptoms. Many women who seek help for their symptoms do so without any awareness of why they are suffering."

"... the insults, the insinuations, the criticism, and the accusations slowly eat away the victim's self-esteem until she is incapable of situation realistically." p. 10

"Emotional-abuse victims become so convinced they are worthless that they believe no one else could possibly want them." p. 11

"... they stay in abusive situations because they believe there is nowhere else to go. Their ultimate fear is that of being all alone." p. 11

Domination "When you allow yourself to be dominated by someone else, you begin to lose respect for yourself, and you become silently enraged." p. 14

Verbal Assaults "This set of behavior involves berating, belittling, criticizing, name-calling, screaming, threatening, blaming, and using sarcasm and humiliation. This kind of abuse is extremely damaging to the victim's self-esteem and self-image." "...verbal abuse assaults the mind and spirit, causing wounds that are extremely difficult to heal."

Emotional Blackmail "An emotional blackmailer either consciously or unconsciously coerces another person into doing what he wants by playing on that person's fear, guilt, or compassion." p. 16

Unpredictable Responses "An alcoholic or drug abuser is likely to be extremely unpredictable, exhibiting one personality when sober and a totally different one when intoxicated or high. Living with someone who is like this is tremendously demanding and anxiety provoking, causing the abused person to feel constantly frightened, unsettled, and off balance" p. 17

Character Assassination "Character assassination occurs when someone constantly blows your mistakes out of proportion; gossips about your past failures and mistakes and tells lies about you; humiliates, criticizes, or makes fun of you in front of others; and discounts your accomplishments." p. 17

"Gaslighting.... One character uses a variety of insidious techniques to make another character doubt her perceptions, her memory, and her very sanity. An abuser who does this may continually deny that certain events occurred or that he said something you both know was said, or by insinuating that you are exaggerating or lying. In this way, the abuser may be trying to gain control over you or to avoid responsibility for his own actions."

Eldridge, Sherrie. *Twenty Things Adopted Kids Wish Their Adoptive Parent Knew.* Jessica Kingsley Publishers. Dell Publishing. 1999

"... if she doesn't grieve the adoption loss, her ability to receive love or attach emotionally to you and others in meaningful relationships may be seriously hindered."

"Expose your child to other adoptees. Adoptees need to hear one another's stories, for this is another wonderful source of validation. There is a silent bond between us that makes us strong."

"Drs. Brodzinsky and Schechter in *Being Adopted: The Lifelong Search for Self*: "In our experience, all adoptees engage in a search process. It may not be a literal search, but it is a meaningful search nonetheless. It begins when the child first asks, "Why did it happen? Who are they? Where are they now?"

"It is vital to keep in mind that there is no "we and they" mentality in the adopted child's world. Birth parents have always been and will always be a part of her world, whether acknowledge or not. It is we, the adults, who sometimes erect walls of competitiveness and posses-siveness in relating to our child." ".... this is difficult information for some parents of closed and semi-closed adoptions. You may find it threatening to open conversations about the birth family. However, it is essential if you are to be in tune with your child's secret world.""

Eldridge, Sherrie. *20 Life Transforming Choices Adoptees Need to Make - Second Edition*. Jessica Kingsley Publishers. 2015

"This was my first lesson about searching for birth information. Nev-er mention the word "adoptee," for it almost always closes the door for further information. "Genealogical research" is the socially correct term, I later learned."

"And well-meaning religious people remarked, "Why do that? You al-ready know your identity as a child of God.""

===

RESOURCES

Book for parents to explain their child's adoption story using birds as a character.

Brodzinsky, Anne Braff, Ph.D. *The Mulberry Bird An Adoption Sto-ry*. Jessica Kingsley Publishers. 2013

This book gives you three ways to answer strange or odd questions. They give you a quick fix option, an option that raises the hearer's awareness, and food for thought on the take-home message.

Bick, Carol and Baker, M.C. *What Do I say Now.* 2B Publications. 2015.

==

WEBSITES

"New Jersey Adoption Resource Clearing House." *New Jersey Adoption Resource Clearing House,* njarch.org/.

"New Jersey Coalition for Adoption Reform & Education." *NJ-CARE,* www.nj-care.org/.

Original Birth Certificate Process for New Jersey-born adoptees born between 1940 - 2015

http://nj-care.org/wp-content/uploads/2016/05/reg-41-newjersey-original-birth-certificate-application.pdf

Download and complete the application form. Mail it to:

Office of Vital Statistics and Registry

Adoption Request Unit

PO Box 370

Trenton, NJ 08625-0370

(call 609-292-4087 ext. 529 for a hard copy)

You need to include two additional things:

1. Proof of Identity (acceptable forms of identity listed in in the instructions section of the application form)

2. $25.00 check made out to the *State Treasurer of New Jersey*

About The Author

J oi R. Fisher is a passionate Educator, Community Leader, Author, Speaker, and Mother who strives to advocate for adoptees, pro-mote counseling, stimulate conversation on adoption sensitivity, call attention to emotional and psychological abuse, empower the youth, encourage STEM and art education, and provide support to underserved communities. Making the world a better place with an abundance of opportunities through compassionate education has been her vision for the last two decades, but her intrinsic motivation to help people spans a lifetime.

Growing up as an only child, Joi always wanted siblings, who knew that wish would come true forty-six years later following the implementation of the New Jersey Adoptees' Birthright Act in 2017. Ultimately, she wound up with three other siblings: a younger brother and older twin step-sisters. Recently Joi created her own family acronym FABW paying homage to the four families that make up the compassionate woman she is today, and she couldn't be any more grateful.

Joi's debut book titled *Finding Joi: A True Story of Faith, Family, and Love*, is a heartfelt memoir that is specially written for the strong individuals who have been through all sorts of dysfunction but still hold on regardless of what life has thrown at them. To Joi, nothing can rip away your happiness from you forever, even a series of toxic relationships, continual poor self-image, or intense fear of abandonment. In finding joy and serenity in her life, her only wish is to help others do the same. However, not only is she an adoption advocate and talented writer, she also is an entrepreneur having established designs for her own t-shirt company Joi Renee Apparel where she also fitness apparel for her daughter's company Sculpted Turtle Fitness. Never one to set limits on herself, she serves as a Guest Speaker for counselors, social workers and various community organization raising awareness on adoption-related topics and the NJ Adoptees Birthright Act.

Furthermore, Joi R. Fisher obtained her Master's degree in Educational Administration, her Bachelor's degree in Criminal Justice, and holds an array of other certifications.

For Bookings & More Information

Log on to: www.findingjoi.us

www.mindthrivepublishing.com

www.sculptedturtlefitness.com